NATIONAL GEOGRAPHIC

Our World

STUDENT'S BOOK 1

AUTHOR
Diane Pinkley

Unit 0	2
Unit 1 My School	8
Unit 2 My World	24
Unit 3 My Family	40
Units 1–3 Review	56
Unit 4 My House	58
Unit 5 Cool Clothes	74
Unit 6 My Toys	90
Units 4–6 Review	106
Unit 7 My Body	108
Unit 8 I Like Food	124
Unit 9 Animal Friends	140
Units 7–9 Review	156
Our World song	158
Cutouts	159
Stickers	

NATIONAL GEOGRAPHIC LEARNING | CENGAGE Learning

Australia • Brazil • Japan • Korea • Mexico • Singapore • Spain • United Kingdom • United States

Unit 0

Welcome to Our World!

Eddie
the elephant

Polly
the parrot

Mia
the monkey

Freddy
the frog

Hello. I'm Eddie. What's your name?

Hi. My name's Mia.

How old are you, Freddy?

I'm five. How old are you, Polly?

I'm seven. It's my birthday!

Happy Birthday!

1 Look and listen. Say. TR: A2

Colours

red
purple
yellow
blue
orange
black
white
green

2 **Look and listen.** Say. TR: A3

3 **Listen.** Point and say. TR: A4

4 **Work with a friend.** Point. Ask and answer. TR: A5

What colour is it?

It's red!

The Alphabet

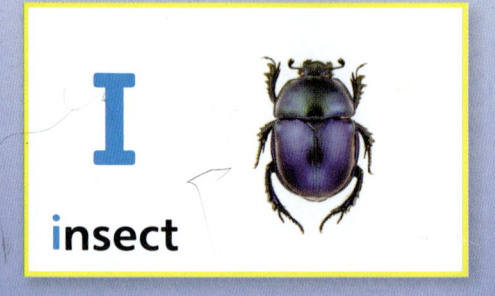

A apple	B baby	C cat
G goat	H hand	I insect
M monkey	N nine	O orange
S sock	T turtle	U umbrella
Y yellow	Z zebra	

D dog
E egg
F fish
J jacket
K kite
L lamp
P pencil
Q queen
R robot
V vegetables
W water
X fox

5 Look and listen. Say. TR: A6

6 **Look and listen.** Say. TR: A7

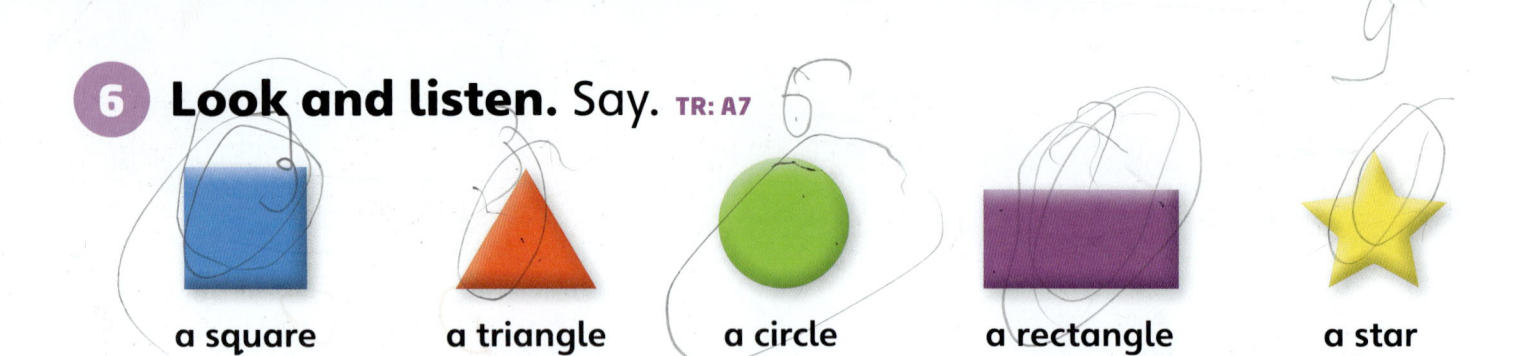

a square   a triangle   a circle   a rectangle   a star

7 **Listen.** Point and say. TR: A8

8 **Look and listen.** Say. TR: A9

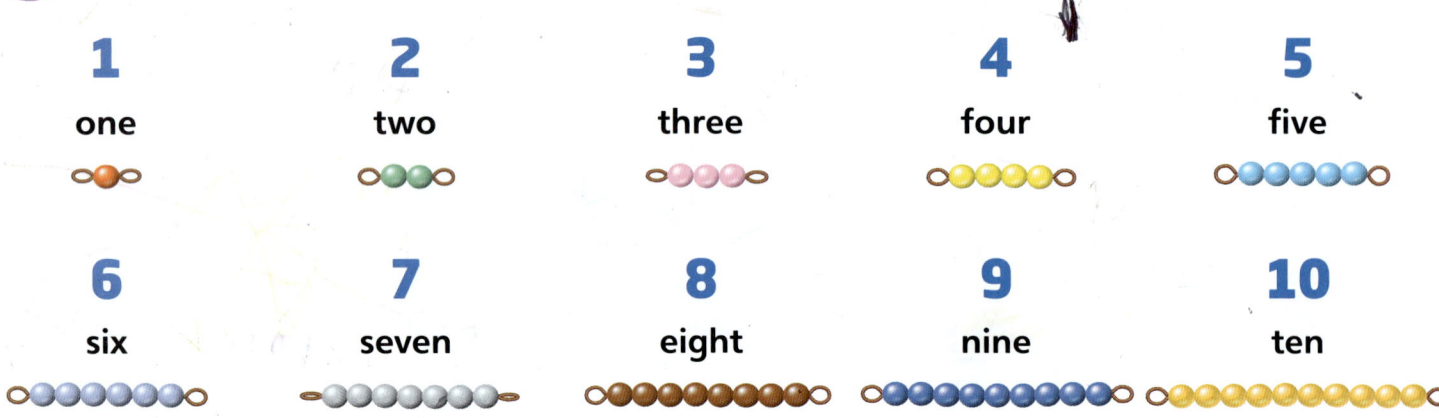

| 1 one | 2 two | 3 three | 4 four | 5 five |
| 6 six | 7 seven | 8 eight | 9 nine | 10 ten |

9 **Listen.** Point and say. TR: A10

10 **Ask and answer.** TR: A11

How many blue squares?

Three.

draw

listen

point

read

say

sing

sit down

stand up

walk

write

11 **Look and listen.** Say. TR: A12

12 **Listen.** Point and say. TR: A13

13 **Listen and do.** TR: A14

Unit 1

My School

In this unit, I will ...
- name classroom objects.
- count classroom objects.
- name colours of objects.

Look and tick.

It's a

☐ book.
☑ globe.
☐ pen.

School in Guilin, China

8

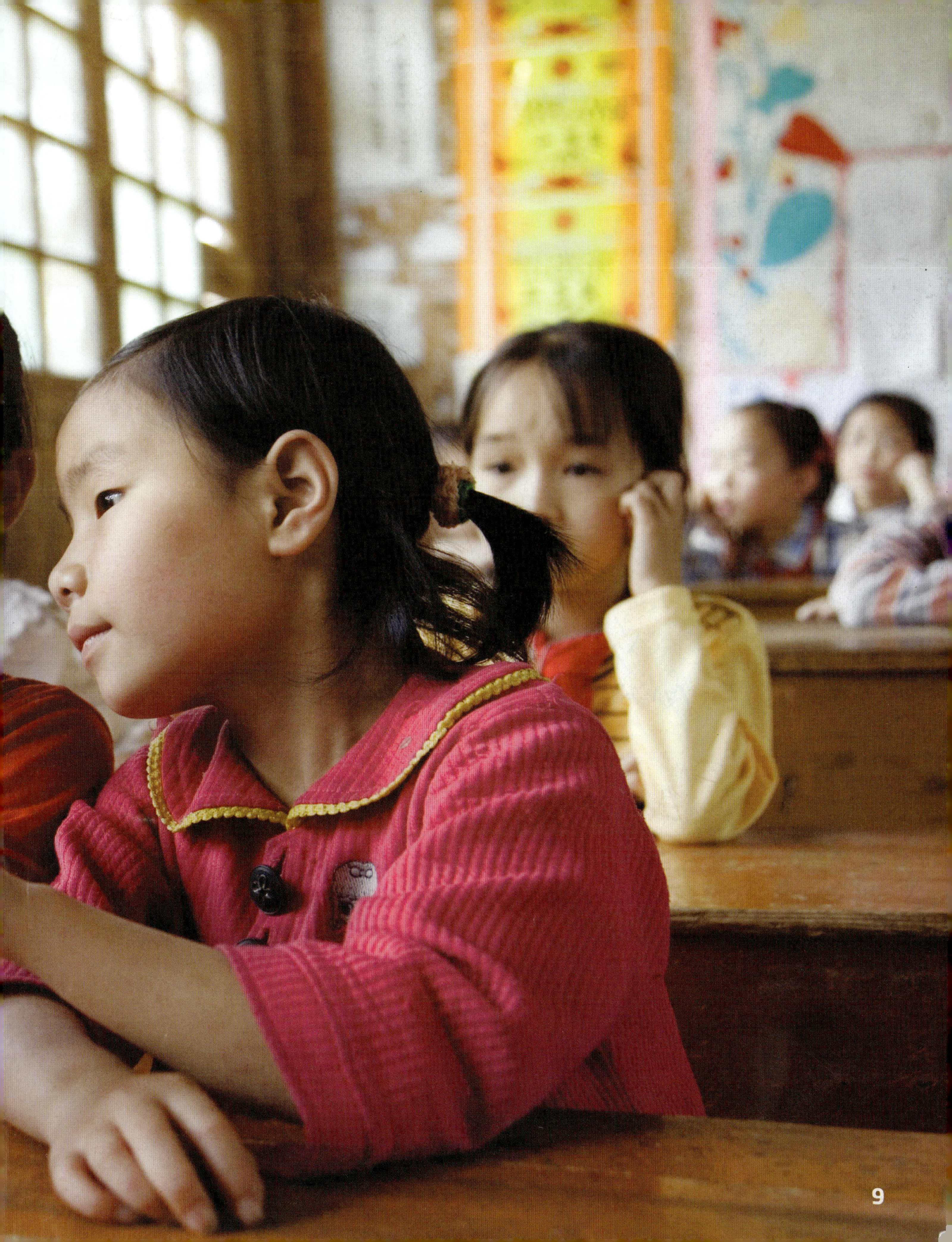

1 **Listen and say.** TR: A15

2 **Listen.** Point and say. TR: A16

a computer

a map

a table

a pen

paper

a classroom

a clock

a pencil

a board

a crayon

3 **Work with a friend.** Point. Ask and answer. **TR: A17**

What is it?

It's a crayon.

11

4 **Listen.** Read and sing. TR: A18

My School

This is my school.
This is your school.
This is my school.
I like my school.

I've got my pencil,
I've got my book.
I've got my pencil.
Come and look!

CHORUS

We can count from one to ten.
Just like this, just like this.

Is everybody ready?
Here we go!
1-2-3-4-5-6-7-8-9-10
Yay!

CHORUS

I know my colours.
Red and blue,
purple, too.
Orange, green and yellow!

CHORUS

I like my school!

5 **Sing again.** Hold up pictures.

GRAMMAR TR: A19

Is it a pencil?   Yes, **it is**.   **It's** a pencil.
Is it a crayon?   No, **it isn't**.   **It's** a pen.

6 **Look.** Listen and (circle). TR: A20

1

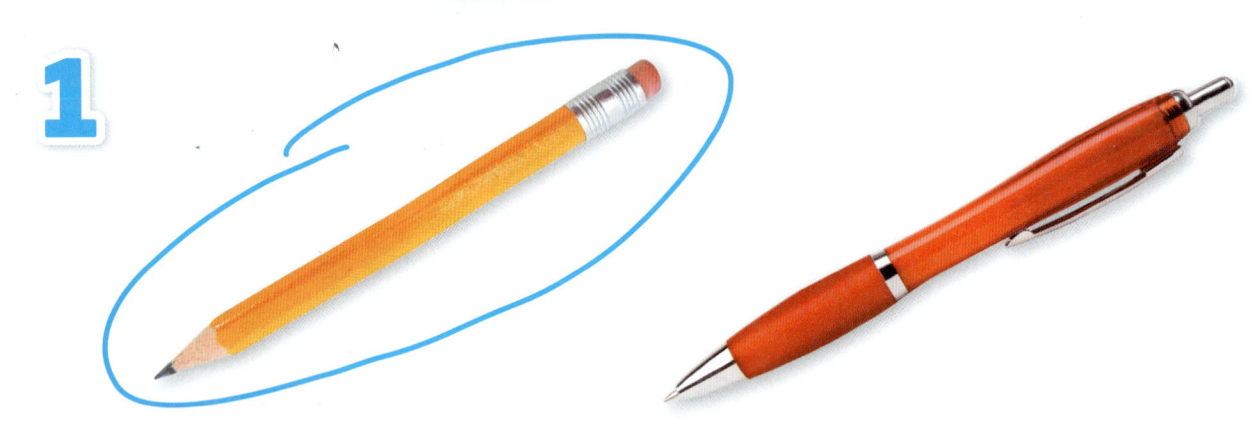

2

3

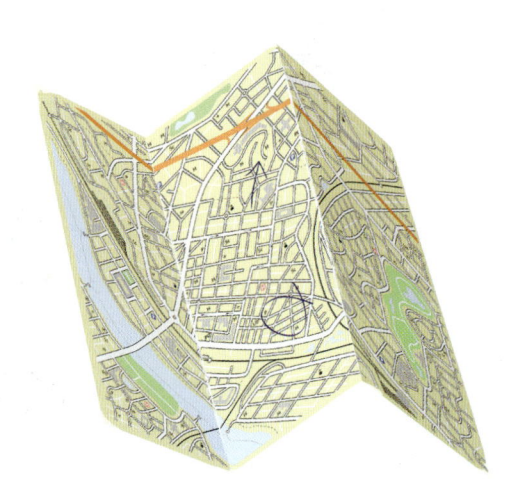

4

5

6

15

7 Listen and say. TR: A21

a book

a rubber

a chair

a desk

a picture

8 Work with a friend. Point and say.

9 Work with a friend. Guess and stick. TR: A22

Is it a desk?

No, it isn't.

Is it a book?

Yes, it is.
It's a book.

16

GRAMMAR TR: A23

What is it?   It's a table.
What colour is it?   It's yellow.
How many pencils?   Three.

What colour is it?

It's yellow.

10 **Work in groups.** Look and point. Ask and answer. TR: A24

11 **Look at the picture.** Write.

1. How many crayons? _There are 3 crayons._

2. What colour is the frog? _The frog is green._

3. How many clocks? _There is 1 clock._

17

12 Listen and read. TR: A25

Cueva de las Manos, Argentina

Drawing and Writing

a wall

a tablet

a hand

a stick

In the past

Now

a canvas

paint

a tablet

18

13 What about you? Circle.

1. I draw on   a wall   (paper).
2. I draw with   a crayon   a stick.
3. I write with   a hand   a pencil.

14 Work with a friend. Look and read. Tick ✓.

	Past	Now
crayon	crayon	✓
hand	hand	
paint	paint	
tablet	tablet	
stick	stick	

15 Look on your desk. Read. Count and write.

1. How many frogs? ___0___
2. How many pencils? _____
3. How many crayons? _____
4. How many sticks? _____
5. How many pens? _____

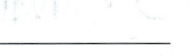

None!

19

16 **Make a name badge.**

1. Cut out the name badge on page 159.
2. Write **Hello** with a crayon.
3. Write **My name is** with a pencil.
4. Write your name in a different colour.

17 **Put on your name badge.**
Walk and talk. TR: A26

Hello. My name is Mia. What's your name?

Hi. I'm Freddy.

NATIONAL GEOGRAPHIC

Our World

Work hard at school.

18 **Look and read.**

I listen. I talk.
I read. I write.

19 **Read and copy.**

I work hard at school.

20 **Make a counting book.**

1. Cut out the pictures on page 159.

2. Decide how many.

3. Colour and glue the pictures.

4. Draw more pictures and write the number.

Now I can …
- ○ name classroom objects.
- ○ count classroom objects.
- ○ name colours of objects.

Look! Six books.

6 books

Unit 2
My World

In this unit, I will …
- name objects in nature.
- name colours in nature.
- talk about nature.

Look and tick.

The boy has got
- ◯ a frog
- ◯ a bird
- ✓ an insect

on his finger.

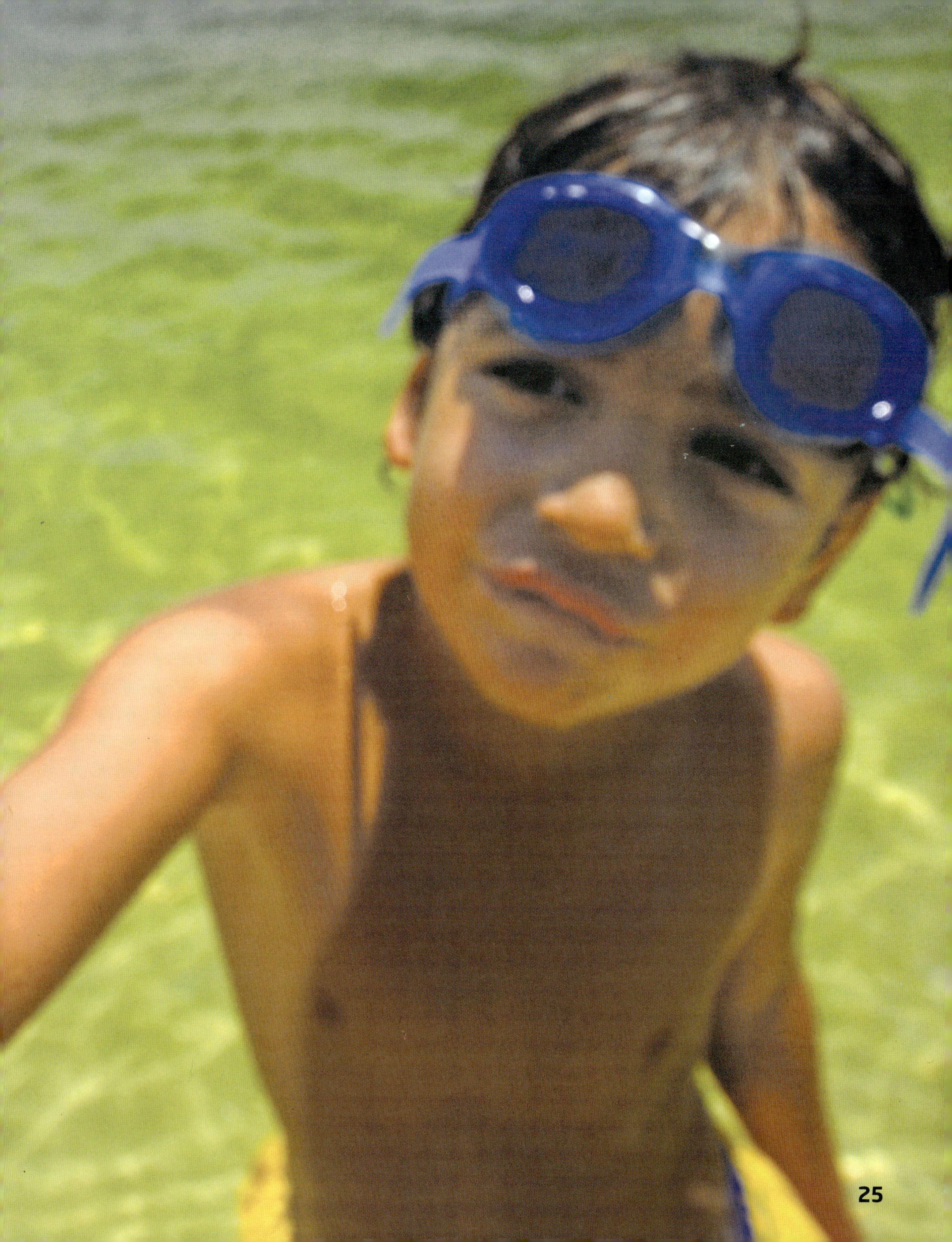

1 **Listen and say.** TR: A27

2 **Listen.** Point and say. TR: A28

the Sun

the sky

the sea

grass

a bird

a rock

a mountain

a butterfly

a tree

a river

3 **Work with a friend.**
Point. Ask and answer. TR: A29

It's yellow. What is it?

It's a bird.

27

4 **Listen.** Read and sing. TR: A30

Nature

Where are the birds?
They're in the sky.

Where are the Sun and the Moon?
They're in the sky.

The sky is part of our world.

Where are the fish?
They're in the sea.

Where are the waves?
They're in the sea.

The sea and the sky
are part of our world.

Where are the trees?
They're in the mountains.

Where are the rocks?
Up in the mountains.

The mountains and the sea
and the sky are part of our world.

What colours can you see
in our beautiful world?
What colours can you see
in our beautiful world?

The colours of the rainbow,
the colours of the rainbow.
The colours of the rainbow,
the colours of the rainbow.

The rainbows and the mountains
and the sea and the sky,
they're part of our world,
part of our world.

Our beautiful world!

5 **Sing again.** Hold up pictures.

GRAMMAR TR: A31

What **is** it? It's a bird.
What **are** they? They're birds.

6 **Look.** Listen and (circle). TR: A32

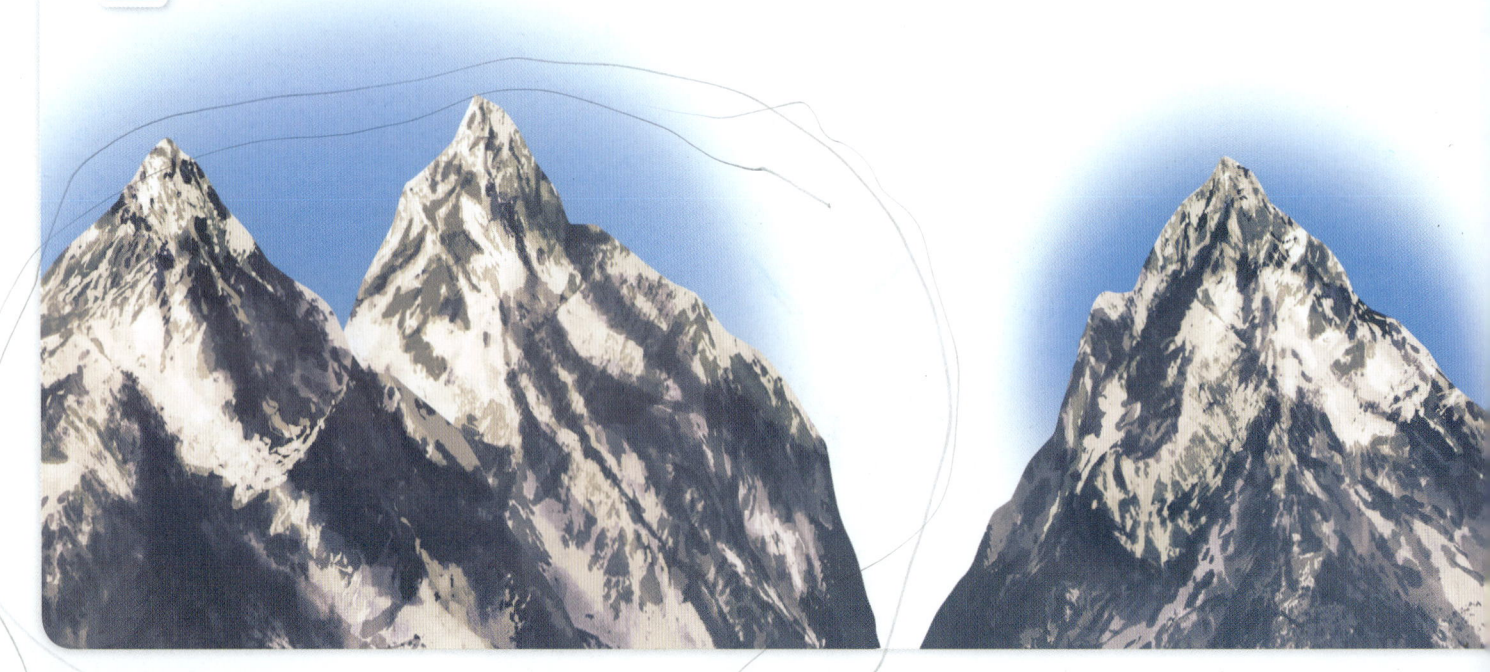

1

2

30

3

4

5

31

7 **Listen and say.** TR: A33

a star

a cloud

the Moon

a flower

a bush

8 **Work with a friend.** Point and say.

9 **Work with a friend.** Guess and stick. TR: A34

Is it a bush?

No, it isn't.

Is it a butterfly?

Yes, it is.

32

GRAMMAR TR: A35

Where is the butterfly?   It's **on** the flower.
Where are the clouds?   They're **in** the sky.

10 Play with a friend. Ask and answer. TR: A36

Where are the clouds?

They're in the sky.

11 Look at the pictures. Write.

1. How many birds? There are 5 birds.

2. What colour is the flower? The flower is Red, Pink, and yellow

3. Where are the stars? The stars are in the sky.

33

12 Listen and read. TR: A37

Rainbows

The sun is in the sky. Rain is in the sky. Look! A rainbow! A rainbow is red, orange, yellow, green, blue, indigo and violet.

13 Listen and read. Circle *yes* or *no*. TR: A38

1. For a rainbow, the sun is in the sky.   yes   no
2. Ten colours are in the rainbow.   yes   no

14 **Colour the rainbow.**

red
orange
yellow
green
blue
indigo
violet

15 **Look.** Circle **things in the sky. Say.**

35

The bush is green.
The flowers are red, yellow and blue.
The birds are red and black.

16 **Colour and write.**

1. The tree is green and brown.

2. The birds is indigo and brown.

3. The flowers are _____.

4. The _____ are _____.

17 **Work in a group.** Talk about your picture.

NATIONAL GEOGRAPHIC

Our World

Enjoy nature.

18 Look and read.

Stop and look.
Enjoy.

Wadi Bani Khalid, Oman

19 Read and copy.

I look at the trees and flowers. I enjoy nature.

37

20 Make a collage about nature.

1 Cut out the pictures on page 161.

2 Draw more pictures.

3 Glue things from nature.

4 Write your name.

38

Look! Two birds are in the trees. They're black.

Now I can …
○ name objects in nature.
○ name colours in nature.
○ talk about nature.

39

Unit 3

My Family

In this unit, I will …
- name family members.
- talk about family members.
- use numbers.

Look and tick.

There are
- ☑ three
- ◯ four
- ◯ five

people in this family.

Bryce Canyon National Park, USA

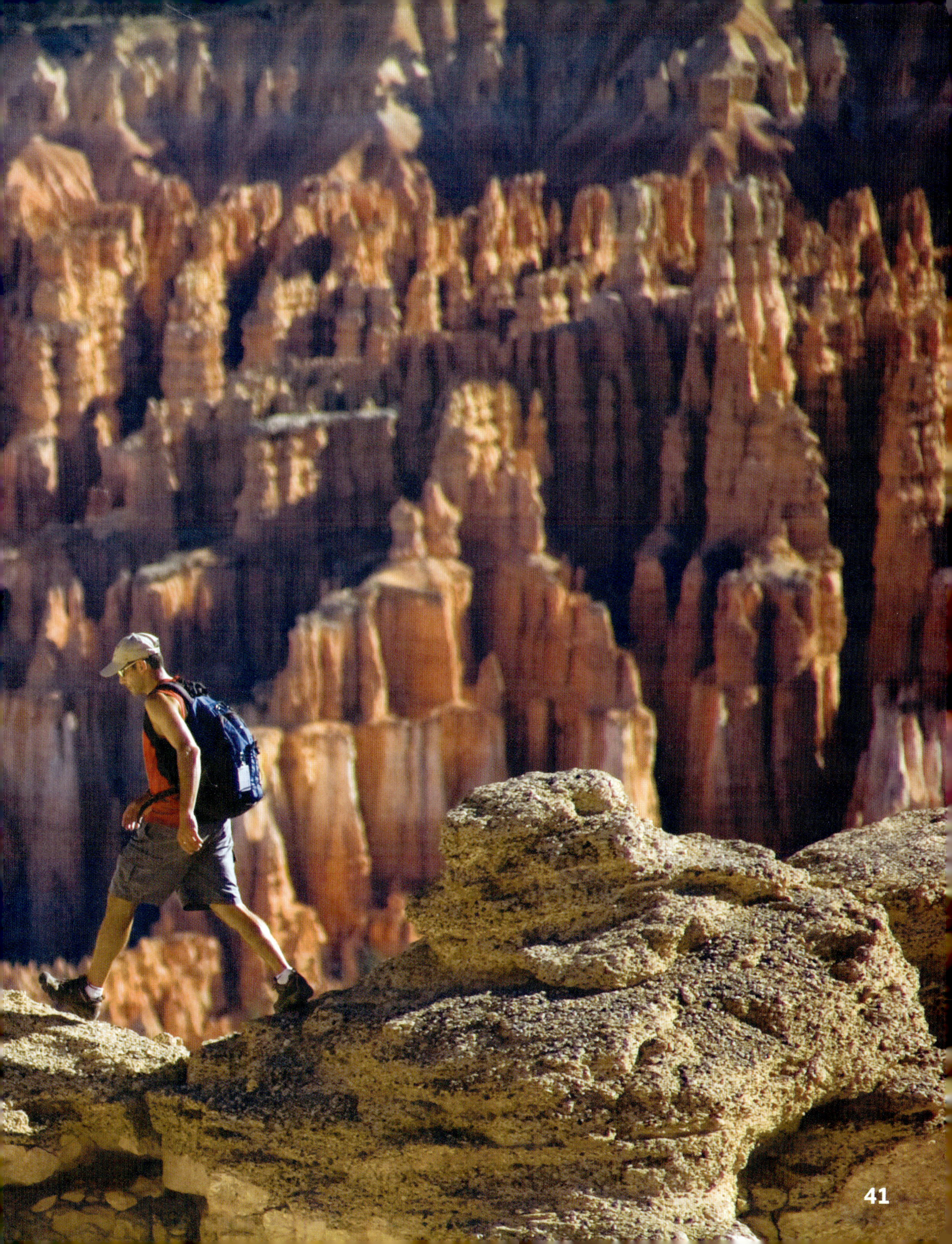

1 **Listen and say.** TR: A39

2 **Listen.** Point and say. TR: A40

my family

parents

mother

brother

father

grandmother

3 **Work with a friend.**
Point and ask about the family. TR: A41

Who's this?

It's the baby.

me

a photo

grandfather

sister

baby

4 Listen. Read and sing. TR: A42

Big or Small?

Have you got a big family?
Have you got a big family?
Have you got a big family?
Yes, my family is big!

Have you got a little brother?
Have you got a little sister?
Have you got a little baby
in your family?

I haven't got a little brother,
little sister, baby brother.
My brother is big!

Some are short, and some are tall.
I've got a big family and I love them all!

How many people are in your family?
How many people are in your family?
How many people are in your family?
Two, three, four, five or more?

There are two boys in my family.
There are two girls in my family.

44

There are six people in my family.
And I love them all!

Some are short, and some are tall.
I've got a big family and I love them all!

My family is big.
Your family is small.

I love the people in my family!
Yes, I love them all.
I love them all!
I love them all!

5 **Sing again.** Hold up pictures.

GRAMMAR TR: A43

How many brothers **have** you **got**? I **'ve got** two brothers.
How many sisters **have** you **got**? I **haven't got** any sisters.

6 Look and listen. Draw a line. TR: A44

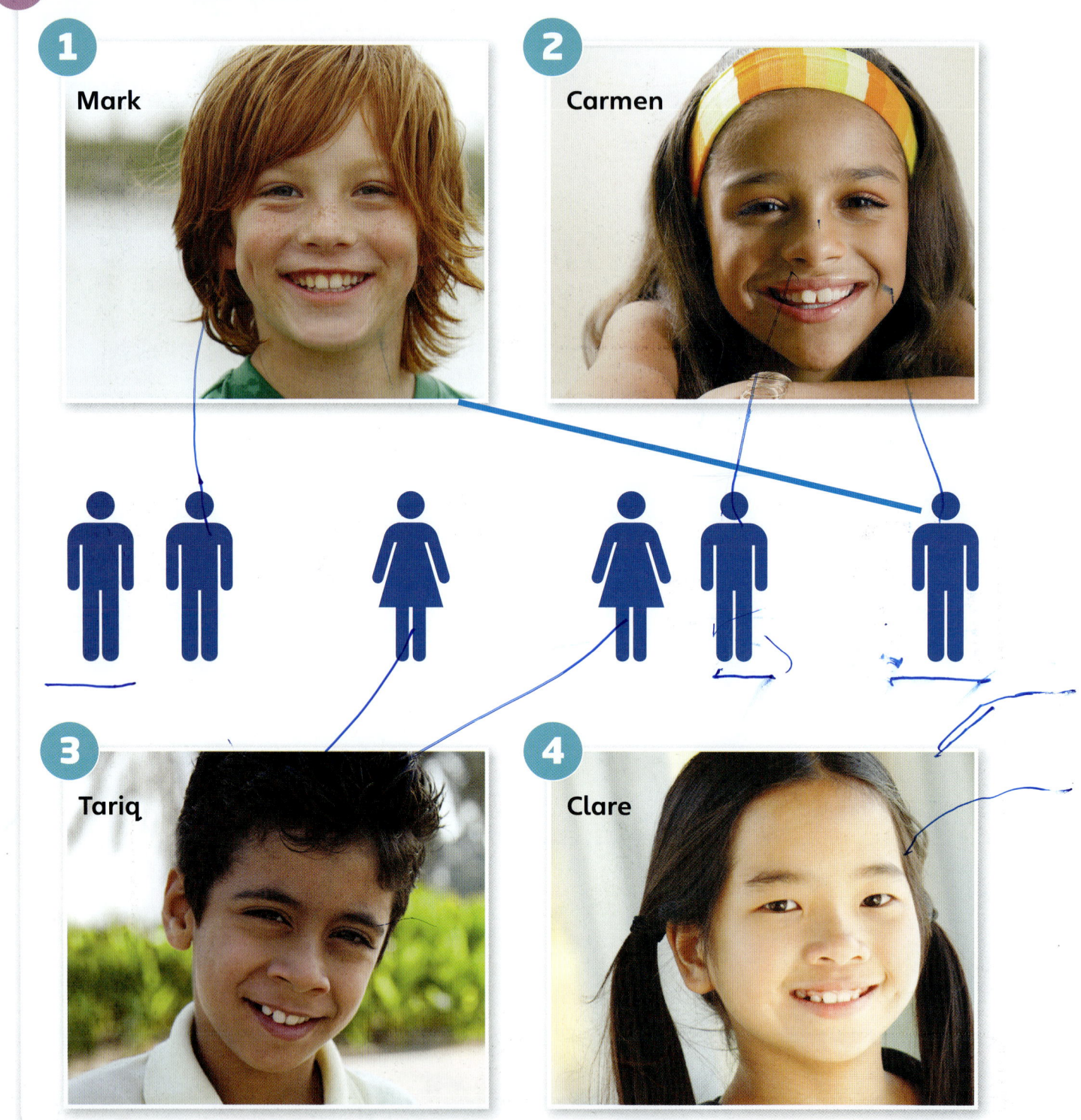

1 Mark

2 Carmen

3 Tariq

4 Clare

46

5 Julia

6 Daniel

7 Ryan

8 Aisha

47

7 Listen and say. TR: A45

young | old | tall | short | small | big

8 Work with a friend. Point and say.

9 Work with a friend. Listen. Say and stick. TR: A46

Number 1. The grandfather is old.

Yes, he's old. My turn.

48

GRAMMAR TR: A47

Who's she?   She's my sister. She's nine.
Who's he?   He's my grandpa. He's old!

10 **Play a game.** Cut out the pictures on page 163. Glue. Listen and play. TR: A48

11 **Look at the pictures.** Write *yes* or *no*.

1. Is the grandfather old? ___yes.___

2. Is the mother tall? ___yes.___

3. Is the brother young? ___yes___

49

12 Listen and read. TR: A49

Families Are Different

This family from Turkey is small. There are parents and a boy.

This family from Mexico is big. There is a grandfather, a grandmother, a father and a mother. There are four brothers and one sister.

13 **Listen and read.** Draw a line. TR: A50

1. The family from Mexico   has got three people.
2. The family from Turkey   has got nine people.

14 **Look at this family tree.** Write.

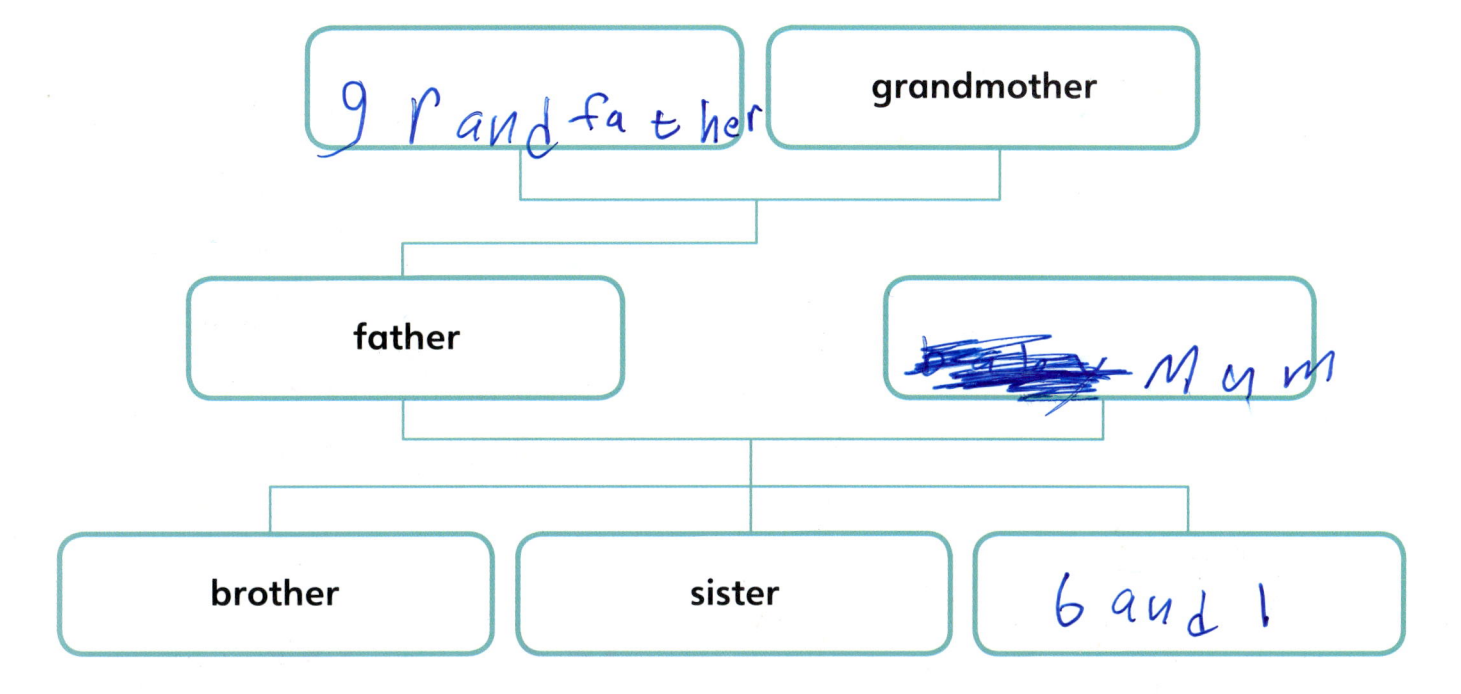

- grandfather — grandmother
- father — Mum (scribbled out)
- brother | sister | 6 and 1

15 **Work with a friend.** Ask and answer. Write.

My family is big.

	You	Your friend
Name	Sarah	Lisa
Family size	10	6
Brothers	6	1
Sisters	1	1

51

I'm Adrian. I've got a big family. In this photo, you can see my grandfather, my grandmother, my parents and my other grandmother. I've got one sister and one brother. In this photo, I am the baby!

16 Draw and write.

I'm _sarah_. I've got a _big family_.

In this picture, you see my _Aunty_.

I've got _4 grand Parents_.

17 Work in a group. Talk about your picture.

52

NATIONAL GEOGRAPHIC

Our World

Love your family.

18 **Look and read.**

Work and play together.

19 **Read and copy.**

I work and play with my family.

53

20 Make a family photo poster.

1. Cut out the frame on page 163. Draw more frames.

2. Choose photos.

3. Glue photos and frames.

4. Write.

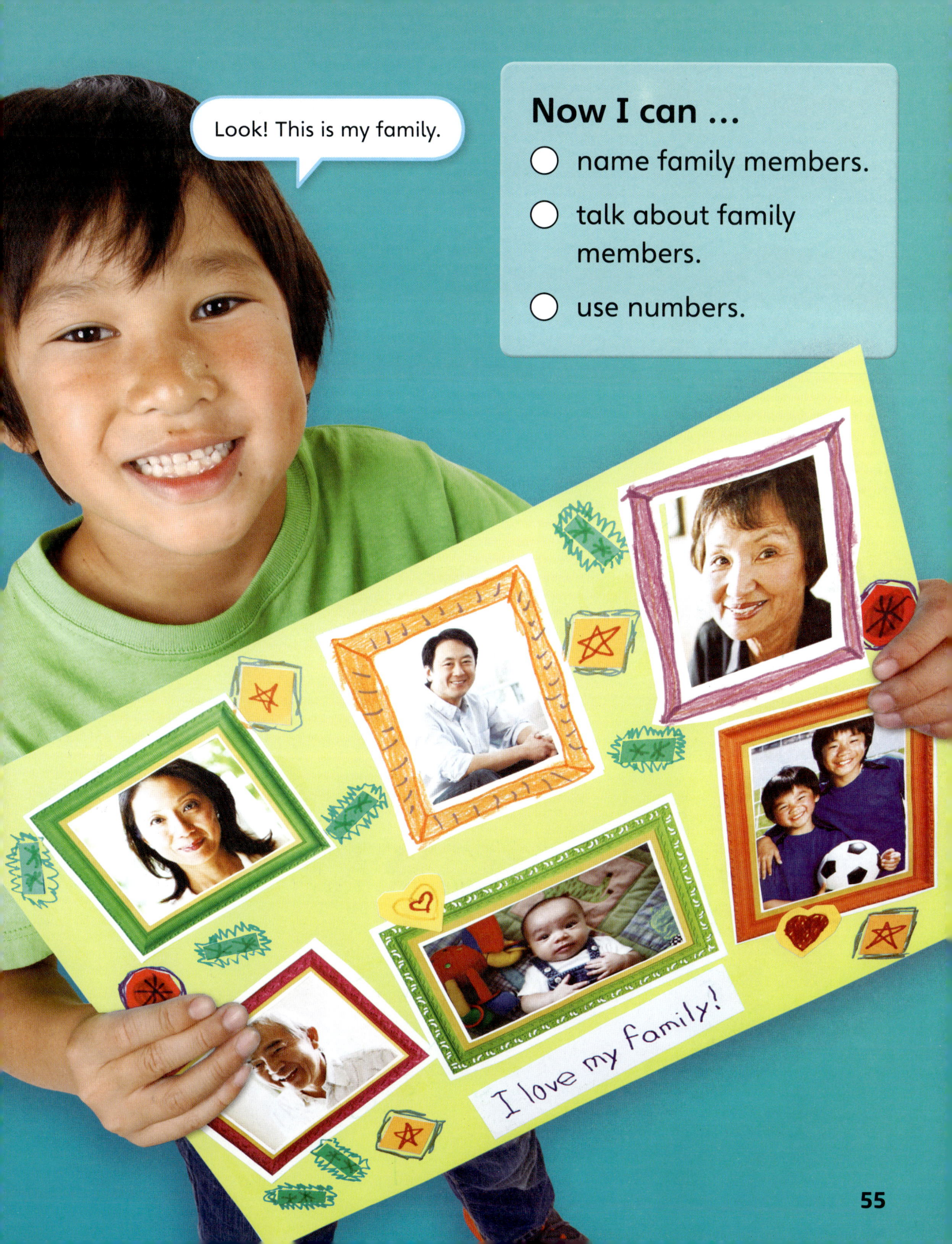

Look! This is my family.

Now I can ...
- ○ name family members.
- ○ talk about family members.
- ○ use numbers.

I love my family!

55

Review

Start

Heads = 1 space
Tails = 2 spaces

56

Finish

Work with a friend.
Look. Ask and answer.

Ask a question!

What is it?

57

Unit 4
My House

In this unit, I will …
- name rooms in a house.
- name furniture.
- talk about actions.

Look and tick.

The house is
- ◯ big.
- ◯ small.

Drina River, Serbia

1 **Listen and say.** TR: A51

2 **Listen.** Point and say. TR: A52

a kitchen

a dining room

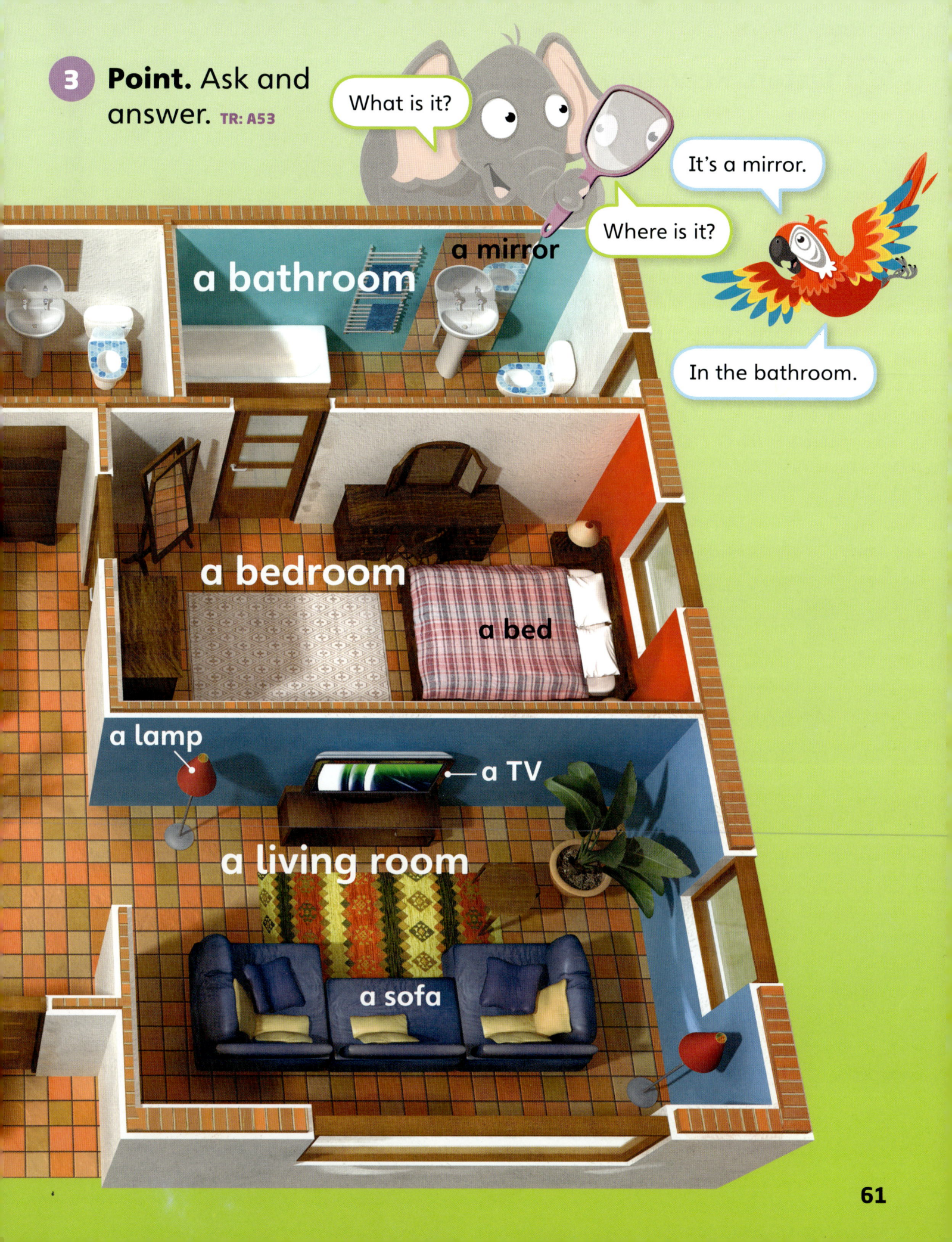

3 **Point.** Ask and answer. TR: A53

What is it?

It's a mirror.

Where is it?

In the bathroom.

a bathroom

a mirror

a bedroom

a bed

a lamp

a TV

a living room

a sofa

61

4 **Listen.** Read and sing. TR: A54

My Home

Where do you live?
I live in a flat.
Where do you live?
I live in a house.

Where do you sleep?
I sleep in the bedroom.
Is there a bed?
Yes, there is.

At home, my home,
at home, where I live.

Where do you eat?
I eat in the kitchen.
Is there a spoon?
Yes, there is.

Where do you play?
I play in the garden.
Is there a ball?
Yes, there is.

At home, my home,
at home, where I live.
It's where I live!

5 **Sing again.** Hold up pictures.

GRAMMAR TR: A55

Is there a table in the kitchen? Yes, **there is**.
Is there a sofa in the kitchen? No, **there isn't**.

6 **Look.** Listen and tick ✓. TR: A56

1. ✓ yes ◯ no
2. ◯ yes ✓ no
3. ✓ yes ◯ no
4. ✓ yes ◯ no
5. ◯ yes ✓ no
6. ◯ yes ✓ no

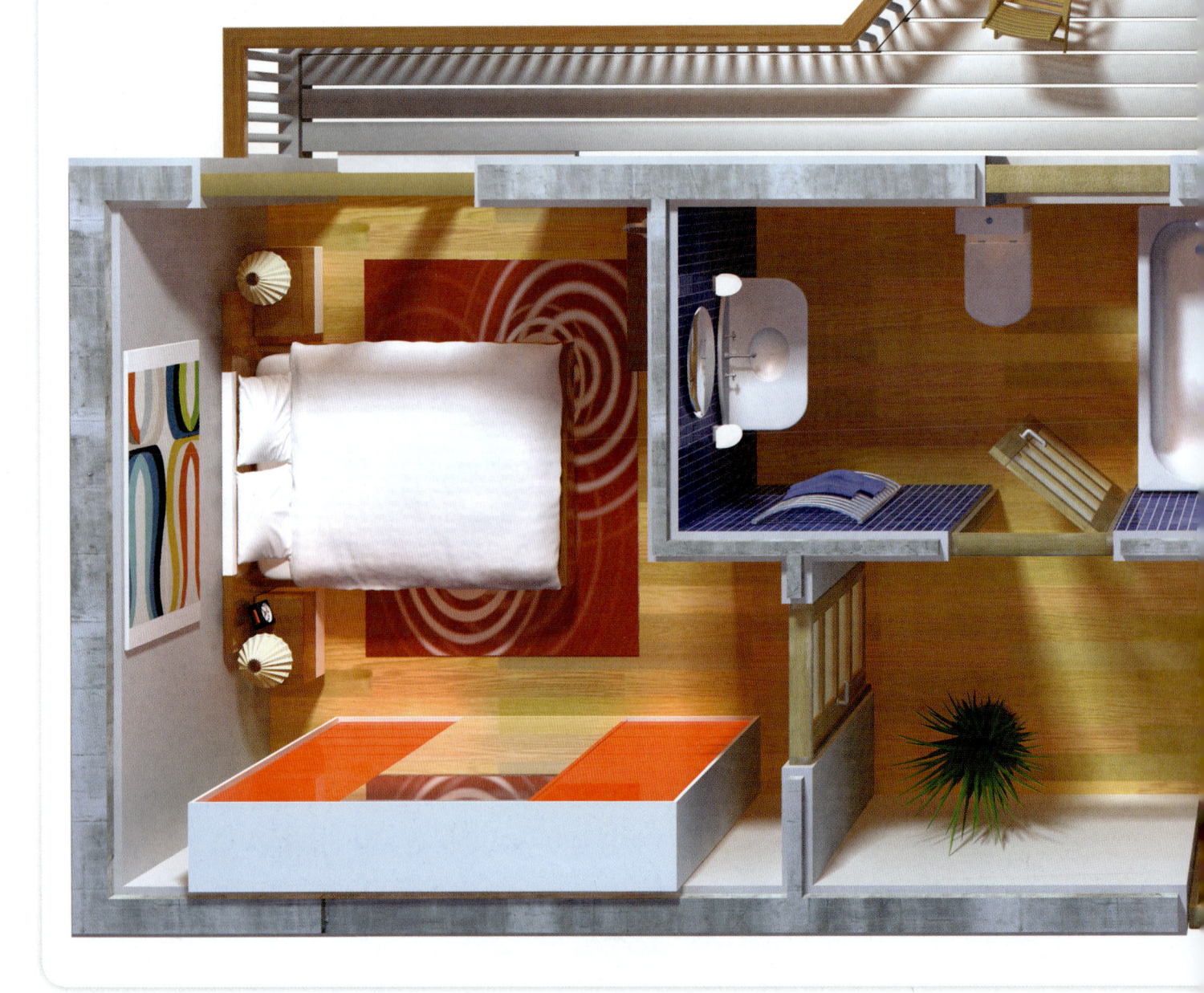

64

65

7 **Listen and say.** TR: A57

sleeping

cleaning

cooking

having a bath

eating

watching TV

8 **Work with a friend.** Point and say.

9 **Work with a friend.** Listen. Say and stick. TR: A58

Number 1. He's cooking.

OK. My turn. Number 2.

GRAMMAR TR: A59

Where's your mother? She's in the kitchen. She**'s cooking**.
Where's your brother? He's in the living room. He**'s watching TV**.

10 **Play a game.**
Point. Ask and answer. TR: A60

Where's the frog?

He's in the dining room. He's eating.

11 **Look at the pictures.** Write.

1. How many frogs are there? _There are eight frogs._

2. What colour is the sofa? _The sofa is orange_

3. Where is the TV? _The TV is living room._

67

12 Listen and read. TR: A61

Houses Are Different

Most houses have got kitchens, living rooms and bedrooms inside, but the outside of houses can be very different.

Is there a house here?

a houseboat

Kerala, India

13 Listen and read. Look. Circle. TR: A62

1. Some houses are on water. (yes) no
2. Most houses have got kitchens. (yes) no

14 **Look at the shapes.** Draw a line.

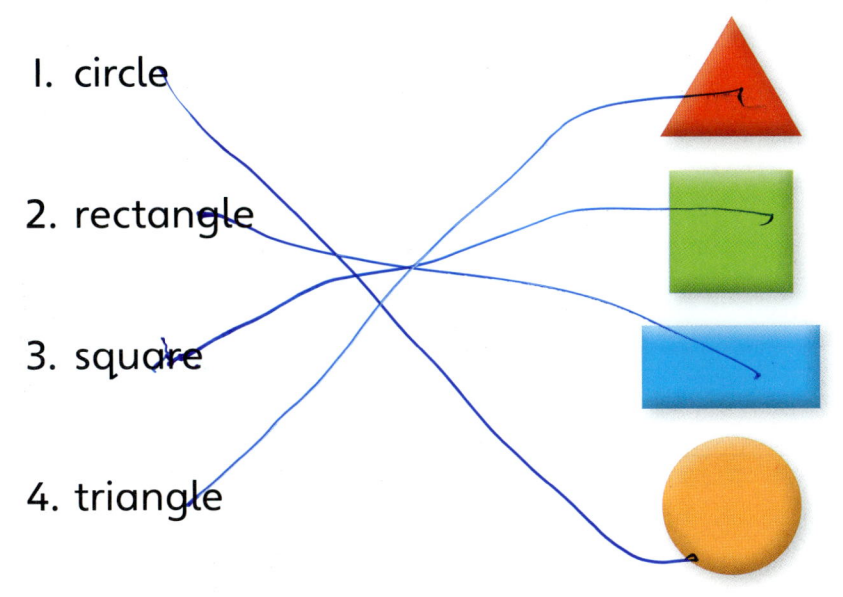

1. circle
2. rectangle
3. square
4. triangle

15 **Look at the houses.** What shape are they? Draw a line.

1. circle   2. rectangle   3. square   4. triangle

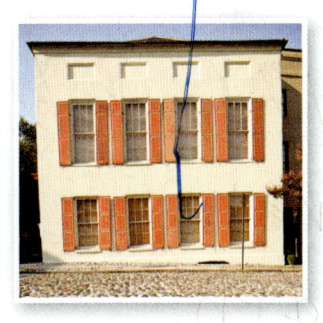

16 **What shape is your house?** Circle.

circle   rectangle   square   triangle

I'm Teddy. This is my bedroom. My bed is blue. I've got a red rug under my bed. There is a lamp on a small table.

Teddy

17 **Draw and write.**

I'm ___Sarah___ This is ___my garden___.

My ___garden___ is ___has a lot of flwers___

I've got ___a Big garden___.

There is ___a tree.___

18 **Work in a group.** Talk about your picture.

70

NATIONAL GEOGRAPHIC

Our World

Be neat.

19 Look and read.

Be neat.
Tidy your room.

20 Read and copy.

I am neat. I tidy my room.

21 Make a plan of rooms in a house.

1

Cut out the pictures on page 165. Draw more pictures.

2

Organise the pictures.

3

Glue the pictures.

4

Write your name.

72

Now I can ...
- ○ name rooms in a house.
- ○ name furniture.
- ○ talk about actions.

Look! There is a TV in the living room.

Unit 5

Cool Clothes

In this unit, I will …
- name clothes.
- name colours.
- say what people are wearing.

Look and tick.

Her clothes are
- ○ red.
- ○ white.
- ✓ blue.

Guatemalan girl

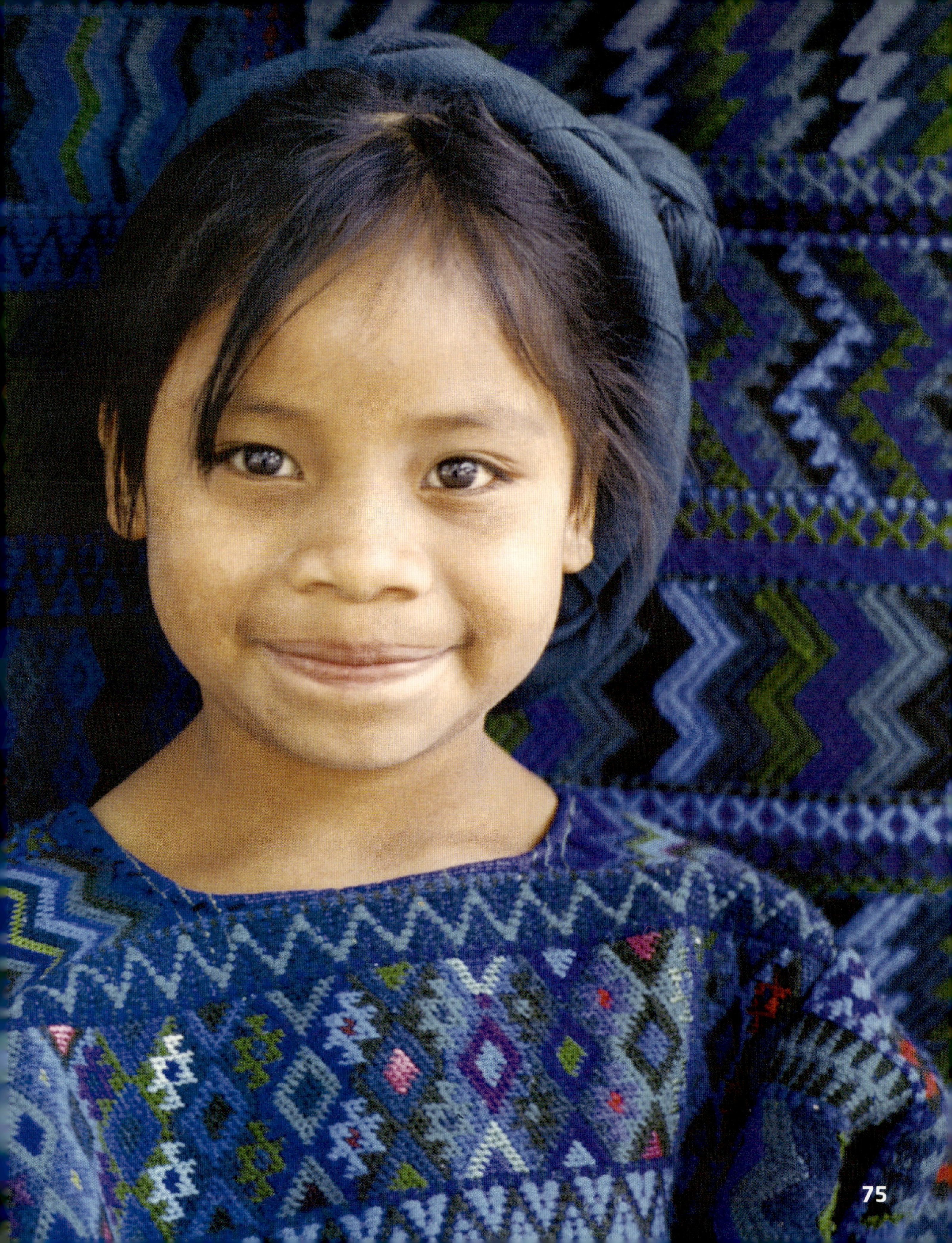

1 Listen and say. TR: B2

2 Listen. Point and say. TR: B3

gloves

a skirt

a hat

a jacket

Guilin, China

a dress

trousers

a shirt

a T-shirt

socks

shoes

3 **Point.** Ask and answer. TR: B4

What are they?

They're shoes. You're wearing shoes.

77

4 **Listen.** Read and sing. TR: B5

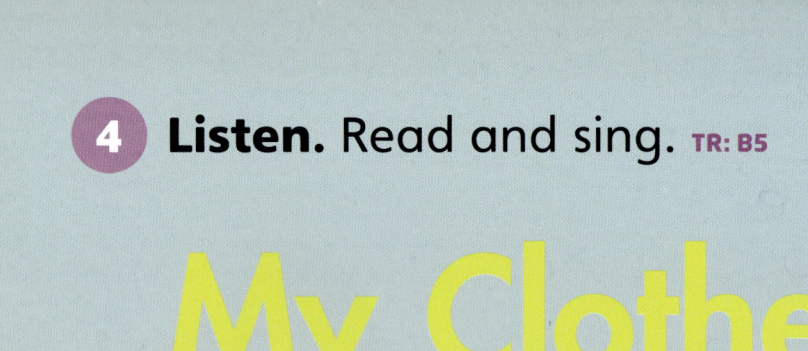

My Clothes

What are you wearing?
What are you wearing?
I'm wearing my brown shoes,
and I really like them.

What are you wearing?
What are you wearing?
I'm wearing my purple hat,
and I really like it.

I like my shoes!
I like my hat!
I like my shirt!
I like my skirt!

What are you wearing?
What are you wearing?
I'm wearing my orange shirt,
and I really like it.

What are you wearing?
What are you wearing?
I'm wearing my pink skirt,
and I really like it.

CHORUS

Oh, you look nice.
Thank you.
Nice hat.
Nice shoes.
Nice shirt.

5 **Sing again.**
Hold up pictures.

GRAMMAR TR: B6

What **are** you **wearing**?   I**'m wearing** a red dress.
My sister**'s wearing** a green dress.

6 **Listen and find.** Colour. TR: B7

80

7 **Draw and colour.** Now, ask and answer. TR: B8

I have a grey trousers and I have a violet sandals

I am wearing a Tshirt red and orange and yellow and green and blue.

What are you wearing?

I'm wearing a blue T-shirt.

81

8 Listen and say. TR: B9

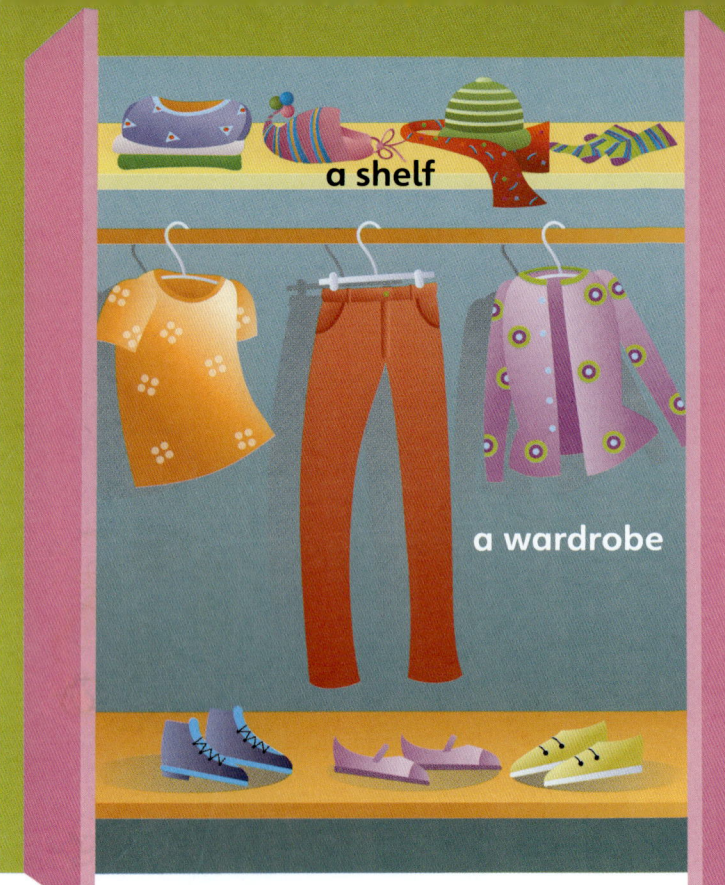

pink

purple

brown

a shelf

a wardrobe

9 Work with a friend. Point and say.

10 Listen and read. Circle. TR: B10

1. Is there a black hat?   yes   no
2. Is there a purple hat?   yes   no

11 Work with a friend. Listen. Say and stick. TR: B11

Where's the green hat?

It's on the shelf. My turn.

82

GRAMMAR TR: B12

What's that?   That's my orange T-shirt.
What are those?   Those are my purple shoes.

12 Play a game. Ask and answer. Draw lines. TR: B13

What are those?

Those are socks.

13 Look at the pictures. Write.

1. What colour are the gloves? _The gloves are blue._
2. What colour is the hat? _The hat is pink_
3. Is there a jacket? _No there isn't a jacket_

83

14 **Listen and read.** TR: B14

Clothes Are Fun!

People all over the world wear special clothes on special days. Sometimes they are clothes from the past.

South Korea

Turkey

Peru

15 **Listen and read.** Look. Circle *yes* or *no*. TR: B15

1. The children from Turkey are wearing shoes. yes no

2. The girls from South Korea are wearing dresses. yes no

16 **Look at Activity 14.** Tick ✔ the costume colours.

	from Turkey	from Peru	from South Korea		from Turkey	from Peru	from South Korea
black				pink			
blue				purple			
brown				red			
green				yellow			
orange				white			

17 **Look.** Draw a line.

1. hat
2. jacket
3. trousers
4. shirt
5. dress

Spain

18 **Work with a friend.** What are you wearing today? Ask and answer. TR: B16

What are you wearing?

I'm wearing a white shirt, blue trousers and black shoes.

85

The girl is wearing a red shirt and a black and red skirt. The boy is wearing a white shirt, a blue jacket and brown trousers.

19 Colour and write.

The girl is wearing _____.

The boy is wearing _____.

20 Work in a group. Talk about your picture.

86

NATIONAL GEOGRAPHIC

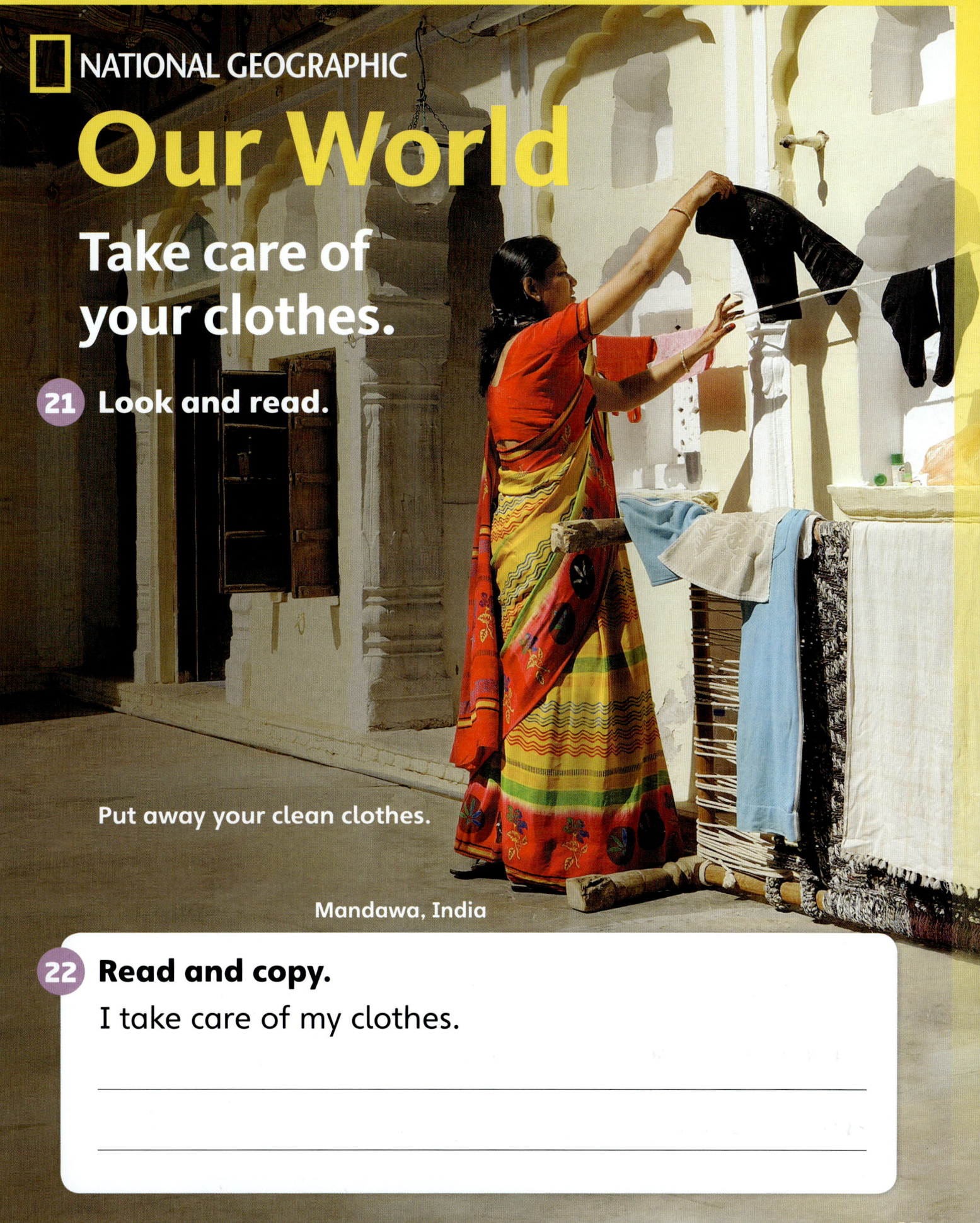

Our World

Take care of your clothes.

21 **Look and read.**

Put away your clean clothes.

Mandawa, India

22 **Read and copy.**
I take care of my clothes.
_____
_____

23 **Dress a stick puppet.**

1 Cut out the pictures on page 167.

2 Choose a head.

3 Glue the clothes.

4 Glue the puppet to the stick.

88

Now I can …
- ○ name clothes.
- ○ name colours.
- ○ say what people are wearing.

He is wearing a blue T-shirt.

Unit 6
My Toys

In this unit, I will …
- name and describe toys.
- talk about wants.
- talk about possession.

Look and circle.
The toys are
blue.   green.
red.   yellow.
black. pink.

Santa Fe, New Mexico

1 **Listen and say.** TR: B17

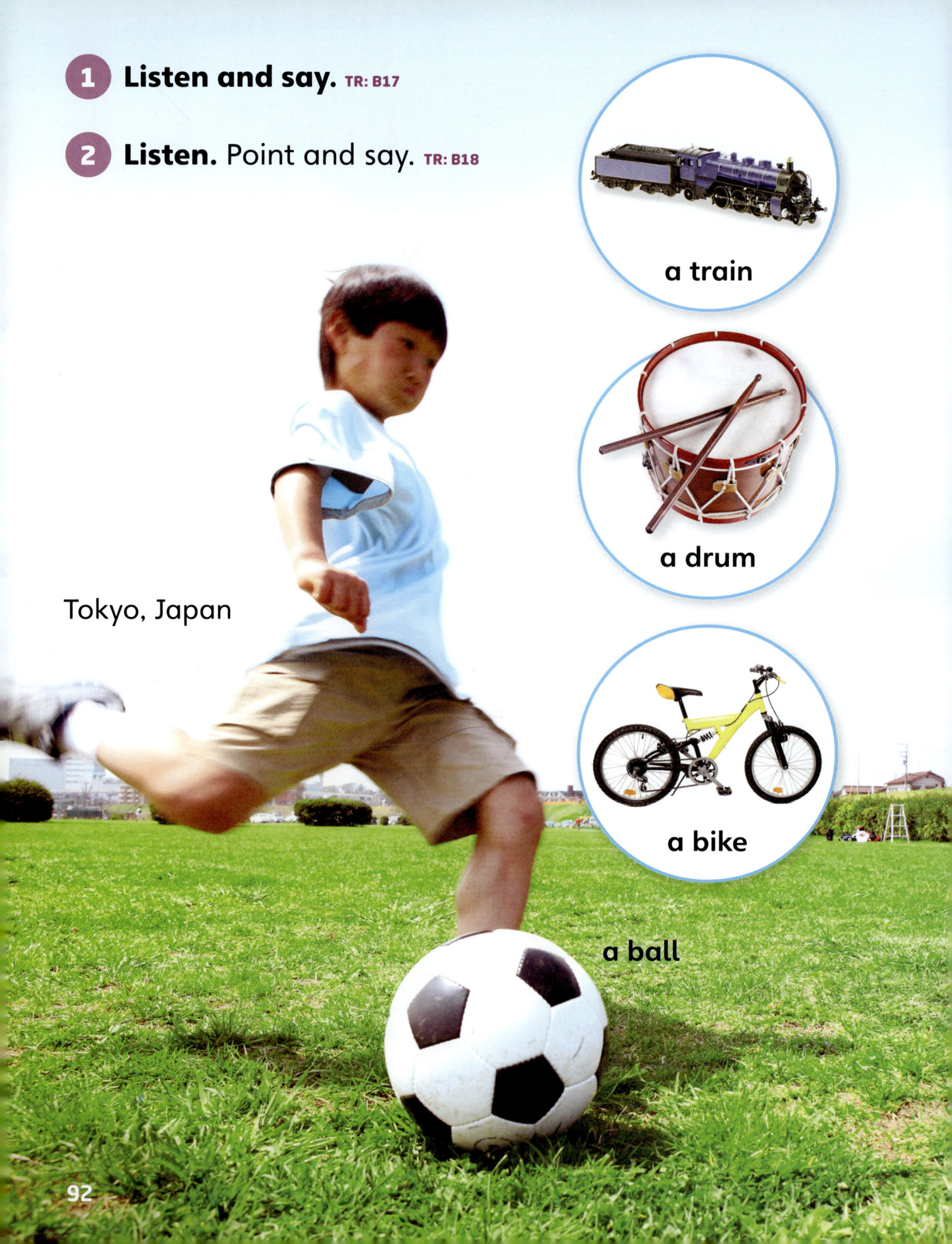

2 **Listen.** Point and say. TR: B18

a train

a drum

Tokyo, Japan

a bike

a ball

a lorry

a kite

a car

a computer game

a top

3 **Point.** Ask and answer. TR: B19

What is it?

It's a ball.

a puppet

93

4 **Listen.** Read and sing. TR: B20

Let's Play!

Do you want to play?
Do you want to play with me?
Do you want to play?
Do you want to play with me?
Do you want to play?
Do you want to play with me?
Yes, I do! Yes, I do!

Do you want to bang on a drum?
No, I don't.
Do you want to ride a bike?
No, I don't.
Do you want to fly a kite?
Yes, I do.
I want to fly my kite with you!

**There is a shelf on the wall,
a box on the shelf,
toys in the box.
Toys for girls and boys!**

Do you want to dress my doll?
No, I don't.
Do you want to kick a ball?
No, I don't.
Do you want to play with trains?
Yes, I do.
I want to play with you!
Choo choo choo!

CHORUS

Let's play!

5 **Sing again.** Hold up pictures.

GRAMMAR TR: B21

Do you **want** a kite? No, I **don't**.
Do you **want** a puppet? Yes, I **do**.

6 **Listen and find.** Draw a line. TR: B22

GRAMMAR TR: B23

Does she **want** a ball?   Yes, she **does**.
Does he **want** a ball?   No, he **doesn't**. He **wants** a lorry.

7 Listen and (circle). TR: B24

1. Yes, he does. He wants a train.

   (No, he doesn't. He wants a drum.)

2. Yes, she does. She wants a puppet.

   No, she doesn't. She wants a car.

3. Yes, he does. He wants a computer game.

   No, he doesn't. He wants a kite.

4. Yes, she does. She wants a top.

   No, she doesn't. She wants a ball.

97

8 Listen and say. TR: B25

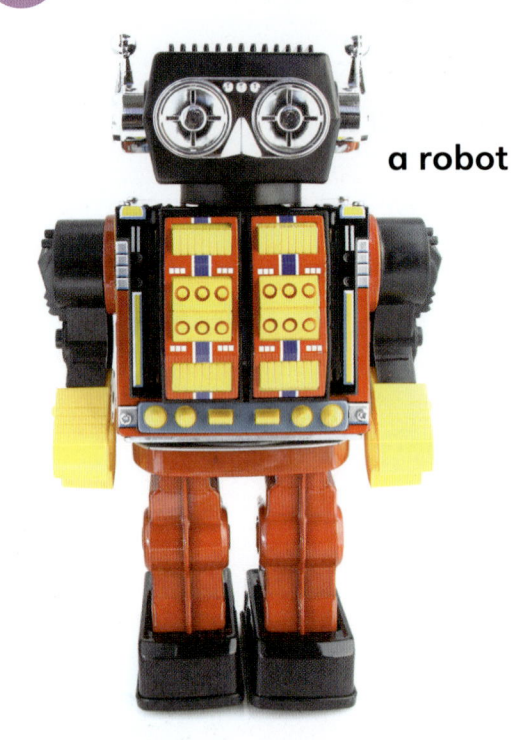

a robot

a teddy bear

a jigsaw

a board game

a doll

9 Work with a friend. Point and say.

10 Look. Listen and read. Circle *yes* or *no*. TR: B26

1. Does he want a robot?   yes   no
2. Does he want a jigsaw?   yes   no

11 Work with a friend. Listen. Say and stick. TR: B27

Number 1. I've got a board game.

I haven't. I've got a robot. Number 2.

1   2   3   4   5

98

GRAMMAR TR: B28

Is this your teddy bear? No, **it isn't**. It's Sonia's teddy bear.
Are these your puppets? No, **they aren't**. They're Mark's puppets.

SHOW AND TELL TODAY

12 **Look.** Listen and read. Tick ✔ yes or no. TR: B29

	yes	no
1. Is this Anna's jigsaw?	○	○
2. Are these Ben's robots?	○	○

13 **Play a game.** Cut out the cards on page 169. Ask and answer. Play with a friend. TR: B30

Are these your tops?

No, they aren't. They're Tina's tops.

99

14 Listen and read. TR: B31

We ❤ Teddy Bears

People around the world love teddy bears. Children play with them and sleep with them. There are even teddy bear museums! This popular museum is in Korea. It's got big bears and small bears, girl bears and boy bears. There are teddy bears for everyone!

15 Listen and read. Look. Circle *yes* or *no*. TR: B32

1. There are teddy bear museums.   yes   no
2. This museum is in China.   yes   no
3. It's got big bears and small bears. yes no

16 Look and write.

1. How many teddy bears are small? _____
2. How many are big? _____
3. How many colours are the bears? _____
4. How many have got shirts? _____

17 Work with a friend. What are your favourite toys? Ask and answer. TR: B33

What are your favourite toys?

My teddy bear and my drum.

101

My favourite toy is my doll.
Her name is Kate. She is small.
She is wearing a pink dress.
I play with her in my bedroom.
She sleeps with me in my bed.

18 **Draw and write about your favourite toy.**

My favourite toy is _____

_____

_____.

19 **Work in a group.** Talk about your picture.

NATIONAL GEOGRAPHIC

Our World

Share your toys.

20 **Look and read.**

Share your toys with your friends.

21 **Read and copy.**

I share my toys with my friends.

_____

_____

22 **Make a cup-and-ball toy.**

1. Decorate your cup. Write your name.

2. Make a hole in the bottom of the cup.

3. Pull string through the hole. Tie and stick the string.

4. Stick the string to a small ball. Play!

This is my new favourite toy!

Now I can ...

○ name and describe toys.

○ talk about wants.

○ talk about possession.

Review

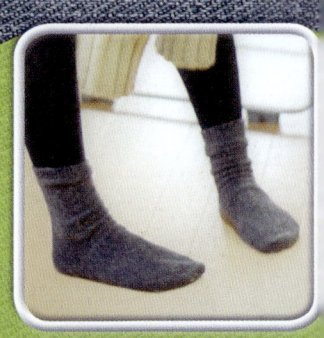

Start

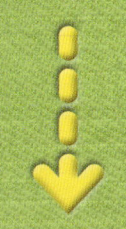

Heads = 1 space **Tails =** 2 spaces

Work with a friend.
Look. Ask and answer.

Ask a question!

Where's the bed?

Finish

107

Unit 7

My Body

In this unit, I will ...
- name parts of the body.
- talk about parts of the body.
- talk about actions.

Look and tick.

This is
- ○ a doll.
- ✓ a boy.
- ○ a girl.

Boy with face painted for a folk dance, Kolkata, India

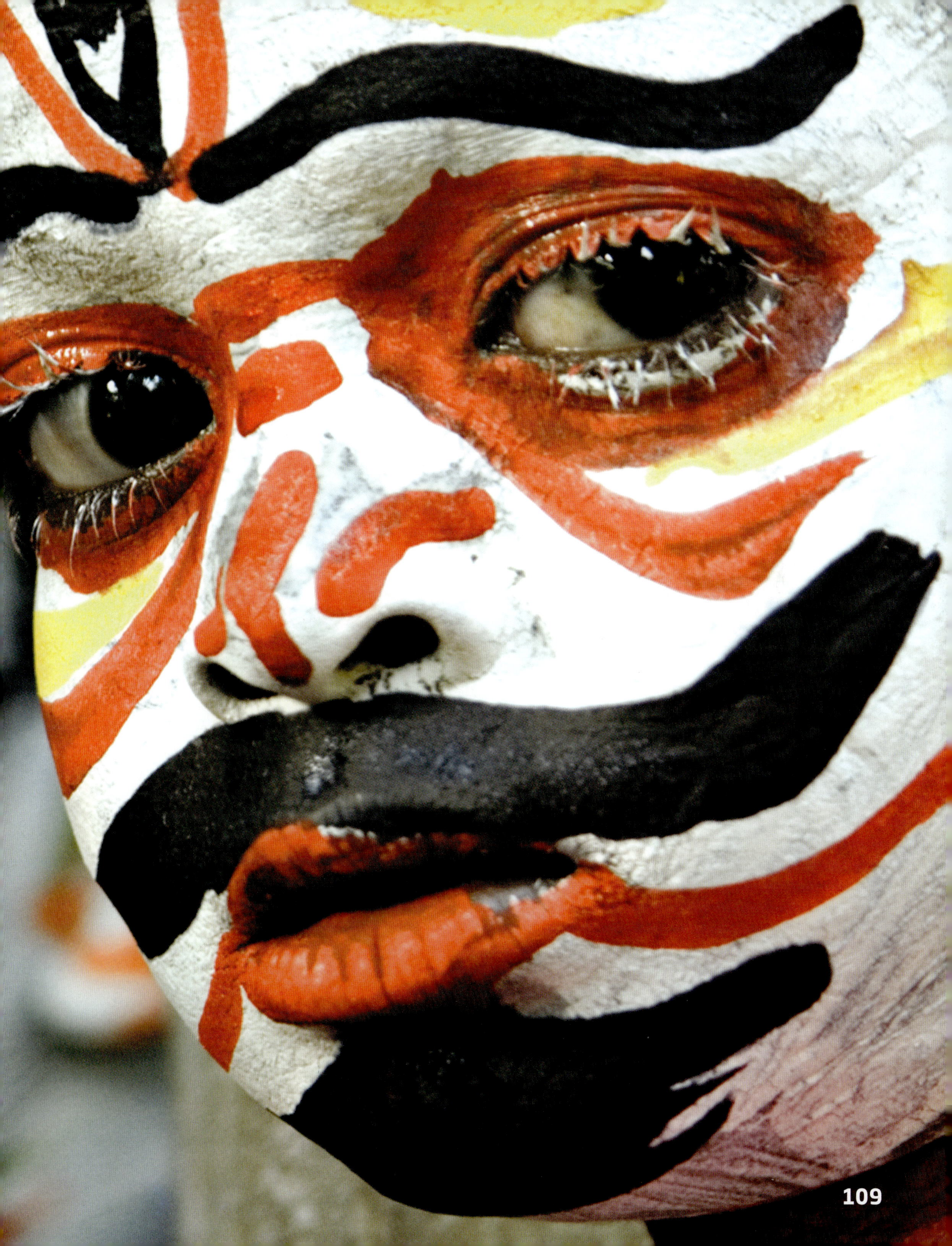

1 **Listen and say.** TR: B34

2 **Listen.** Point and say. TR: B35

a foot

a leg

a neck

a head

an ear
an eye
a nose
a mouth
hair
an arm
a hand
feet

3 **Work with a friend.** Point. Ask and answer. TR: B36

What are these?

They're hands.

111

4 **Listen.** Read and sing. TR: B37

My Body

My body, my body!
It's fun to move my body!
My body, my body!
Can you dance with me?

Legs, legs. Move your legs.
Legs, legs. Move your legs.
Legs, legs. Move your legs.
Can you walk with me?

Feet, feet. Move your feet.
Feet, feet. Move your feet.
Feet, feet. Move your feet.
Can you jump with me?

CHORUS

Mouth, mouth. Move your mouth.
Mouth, mouth. Move your mouth.
Mouth, mouth. Move your mouth.
Can you sing with me?

Hands, hands. Move your hands.
Hands, hands. Move your hands.
Hands, hands. Move your hands.
Can you clap with me?

CHORUS

My body, my body!
I love to move my body!
My body, my body!
Can you dance with me?

5 **Sing again.**
Hold up pictures.

GRAMMAR TR: B38

My hair is brown. **My** eyes are brown.
Your hair is brown. **Your** eyes are brown.

6 **Look and listen.** Write the number in the box. TR: B39

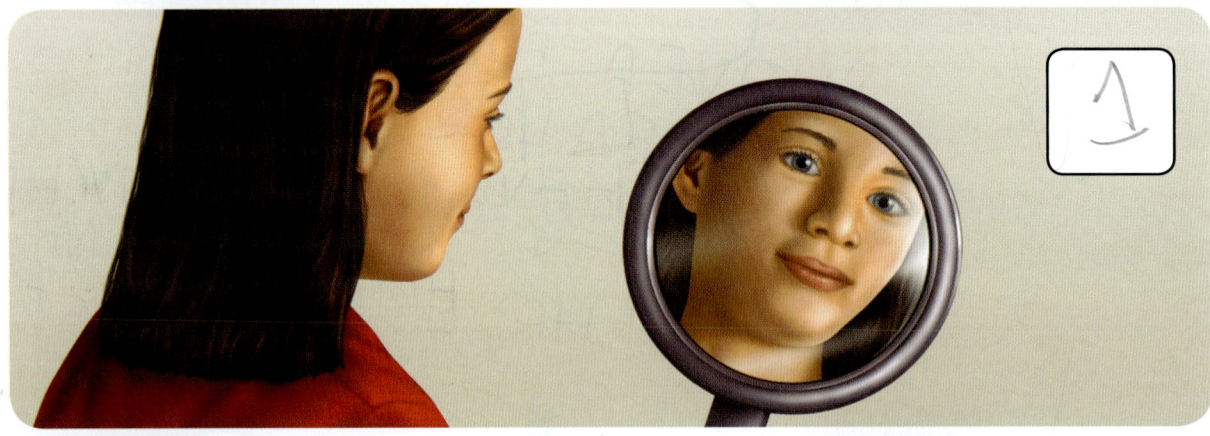

[3]

[1]

[2]

114

GRAMMAR TR: B40

His hair is brown.   **His** eyes are brown.
Her hair is brown.   **Her** eyes are brown.

7 **Look and listen.** Draw a line. TR: B41

1. Her ears are small.

2. His feet are big.

115

8 Listen and say. TR: B42

long hair

strong arms

run

walk

jump

9 Work with a friend. Point and say.

10 Work with a friend. Say and stick. TR: B43

Number 1. Her hair is long.

Yes, it's long. My turn.

116

GRAMMAR TR: B44

I **can** walk.   She **can** jump.
Can you run?   Yes, I **can**. I've got strong legs!

11 **Play a game.** Cut out the pictures on page 171. Glue. Listen and play. TR: B45

12 **Look at the pictures.** Write *yes* or *no*.

1. Can the boy run? _Yes, he can_

2. Can the baby jump? _No he can't_

3. Can the mother cook? _Yes, she can_

117

13 **Listen and read.** TR: B46

Sculptures Are Fun

Some artists draw and paint. Some artists make sculptures. They make people and animals. Look at the man with a hat. His arms and legs are big. His horse's head is small. Look at the balloon dog. Its legs are big. Its ears are long. Artists can make lots of fun things!

Fernando Botero's *Man on Horse*

Jeff Koons's *Balloon Dog*

14 **Listen and read. Circle.** TR: B47

1. There are **two** / **three** sculptures.
2. Some arms and legs are **big** / **old**.
3. We can see a dog with **long** / **short** ears.

15 **Read and tick ✔.**

Man	legs	arms
big	✔	big
small		

Dog	legs	ears
big	✓	~~~~
long		✓

16 **Look. Circle and write.**

1. My robot **hasn't got / (has got)** hair.

   It **hasn't got / (has got)** __1__ head.

   It **hasn't got / has got** ~~two~~ eyes.

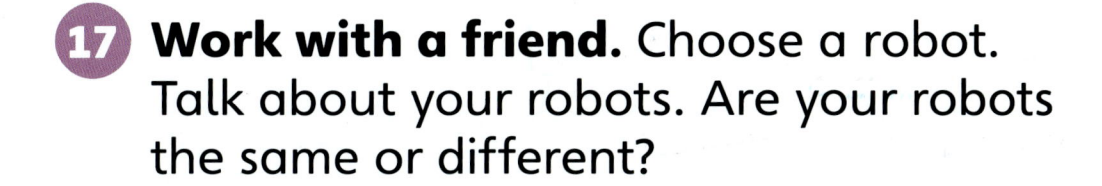

2. My robot **hasn't got / has got** ears.

   It **hasn't got / has got** _two_ big hands.

   It **hasn't got / has got** _two_ short legs.

3. My robot **hasn't got / has got** __2__ eyes.

   It **hasn't got / has got** _2_ long arms.

   It **hasn't got / has got** _1_ leg.

17 **Work with a friend.** Choose a robot. Talk about your robots. Are your robots the same or different?

119

I'm Antoni. I've got two eyes, one nose and one mouth. I've got two arms and two legs. I like spiders. My spider costume has got eight eyes and eight legs. I'm a cool spider!

18 **Draw a costume and write.**

I'm HAPPY . I've got 4 legs .
I've got 2 heacb fish's tail .
My _____ costume has got _____
_____.

19 **Work in a group.** Talk about your picture.

NATIONAL GEOGRAPHIC

Our World

Be clean.

20 Look and read.

Wash your hands.
Wash your body.
Brush your teeth.

21 Read and copy.

I wash my body. I am clean.

_____

_____

22 **Make a robot.** Work with a friend.

1 Cut out the body.

2 Cut out a card.

3 Write the numbers.

4 Cut out or draw parts. Glue them.

Look! Our robot has got two heads!

Now I can ...

- ○ name parts of the body.
- ○ talk about parts of the body.
- ○ talk about actions.

Unit 8
I Like Food

In this unit, I will ...
- name food.
- talk about likes and dislikes.
- talk about my favourite food.

Look and tick.

The lady sells
- ◯ flowers.
- ✓ fruit.
- ◯ vegetables.

Kasbah, Rabat, Morocco

1 **Listen and say.** TR: B48

2 **Listen.** Point and say. TR: B49

a banana

pizza

a salad

an apple

an orange

126

rice

soup

an egg

a sandwich

chicken

fish

a biscuit

3 **Work with a friend.**
Point. Ask and answer. TR: B50

What is it?

It's an orange.

127

4 Listen. Read and sing. TR: B51

Yes, Please!

Pizza?
I like pizza!
Yes, I do! Yes, I do! Yes, I do!
I like pizza!
Yes, I do!
I like it very much!

Apples?
I like apples!
Yes, I do! Yes, I do! Yes, I do!
I like apples!
Yes, I do!
I like them very much!

Do you want a biscuit?
Do you want some cheese?
Do you want a banana?
Yes, please!

Chicken?
I like chicken!
Yes, I do! Yes, I do! Yes, I do!
I like chicken!
Yes, I do!
I like it very much!

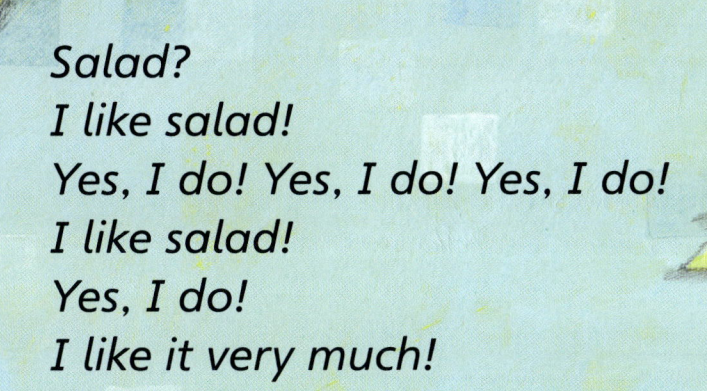

Salad?
I like salad!
Yes, I do! Yes, I do! Yes, I do!
I like salad!
Yes, I do!
I like it very much!

CHORUS

Oranges?
I like oranges!
Yes, I do! Yes, I do! Yes, I do!
I like oranges!
Yes, I do!
I like them very much!

Water?
And I like water!
Yes, I do! Yes, I do! Yes, I do!
I like water!
Yes, I do!
I like it very much!

CHORUS

Yes, please!
Yes, PLEASE!

5 Sing again.
Hold up pictures.

GRAMMAR TR: B52

Do you **like** apples?   No, I **don't**. I **don't like** apples.
Do you **like** bananas?   Yes, I **do**. I **like** bananas.

6 **What do they like?** Listen and find. Circle and write. TR: B53

1. oranges   2. biscuits   3. Apples

GRAMMAR TR: B54

Do you **like** fish?   No, I **don't**. I **don't like** fish.
Do you **like** chicken?   Yes, I **do**. I **like** chicken.

7 **What do they like?** Listen and find. Circle and write. TR: B55

1. chicken   2. Pizza   3. soup

131

8 Listen and say. TR: B56

tea   orange juice   water   lemonade   milk

9 Work with a friend. Point and say.

10 Look. Listen and read. Circle yes or no. TR: B57

1. Does she like orange juice?   yes   no
2. Does she like water?   yes   no

11 Work with a friend. Say and stick. TR: B58

Number 1. I like water.

I don't like water. I like tea. Number 2.

132

GRAMMAR TR: B59

an apple   **an** egg   **an** orange   **a** banana   **a** biscuit   **a** sandwich

12 Play a game. Play with a friend. Find and say. Draw lines. TR: B60

Look! It's an apple.

That is an apple, too.

13 Look at the pictures. Write.

1. Is there a frog? _No, there isn't a frog._
2. Is there an orange? _Yes there is a orange._
3. Is there a sandwich? _Yes there is a sandwich._
4. Is there a rubber? _No There isn't_

133

14 **Listen and read.** TR: B61

Fun Food

Every day, people eat food. Every day, people play. Some people play with food! They make pictures of people or animals from fruit and vegetables. Some make sculptures. Lots of people like making animals. Some of these animals look real, and some animals look like they are from stories. Some food sculptures look like toys. These are all examples of fun food.

You can eat everything in this picture!

15 **Listen and read.** Look. (Circle) *yes* or *no*. TR: B62

1. People can make sculptures with food. (yes) no
2. People make animals with food. (yes) no
3. Some animals look real. (yes) no

16 **Match.**

biscuit

orange

apple

banana

17 **Look at the photo on page 134.** Write.

1. Are there any trees? _yes there ln·tr̶ees_
2. Are there any people? _yes there are_
3. Are there any houses? _yes there are houses_
4. Are there any clouds? _____

18 **Work with a friend.** Ask and answer.
What are your favourite foods? TR: B63

What are your favourite foods?

Chicken and pizza.

135

I eat my favourite foods at lunchtime and at night. For lunch, I like soup, a cheese sandwich or a chicken sandwich. For dinner, I like salad, fish and rice. My favourite drink is water or lemonade.

19 **Draw and write about your favourite foods.**

My favourite foods are _cucumber and watermelon and rice and orange juice_.

20 **Work in a group.** Talk about your picture.

NATIONAL GEOGRAPHIC

Our World

Eat good food.

21 **Look and read.**

Eat fruit and vegetables.
Drink water and juice.

Cedar waxwing
eating berries

22 **Read and copy.**

I eat fruit and vegetables. I drink water and juice.

_____

_____

23 Make a placemat.

1 Cut out the pictures on page 173.

2 Glue the pictures.

3 Decorate and draw.

4 Write your name.

Now I can ...
- ○ name food.
- ○ talk about likes and dislikes.
- ○ talk about my favourite foods.

These are my favourite foods. I like chicken, rice and salad.

Omar

139

Unit 9

Animal Friends

In this unit, I will ...
- name animals.
- talk about what animals can do.
- describe a favourite animal.

Tick T for *True* or F for *False*.

1. There is a monkey and a cat.   T F ✓
2. The monkey likes the bird.   T F
3. The bird is green.   T F
4. The monkey is a baby.   T F

Macaque monkey and dove,
Neilingding Island, China

141

1 **Listen and say.** TR: B64

2 **Listen.** Point and say. TR: B65

a turtle

a dog

a cat

a frog

a duck

142

a horse

a goat

a cow

a chicken

a rabbit

a sheep

a donkey

3 **Work with a friend.**
Point. Ask and answer. TR: B66

What is it?

It's a donkey.

143

4 Listen. Read and sing. TR: B67

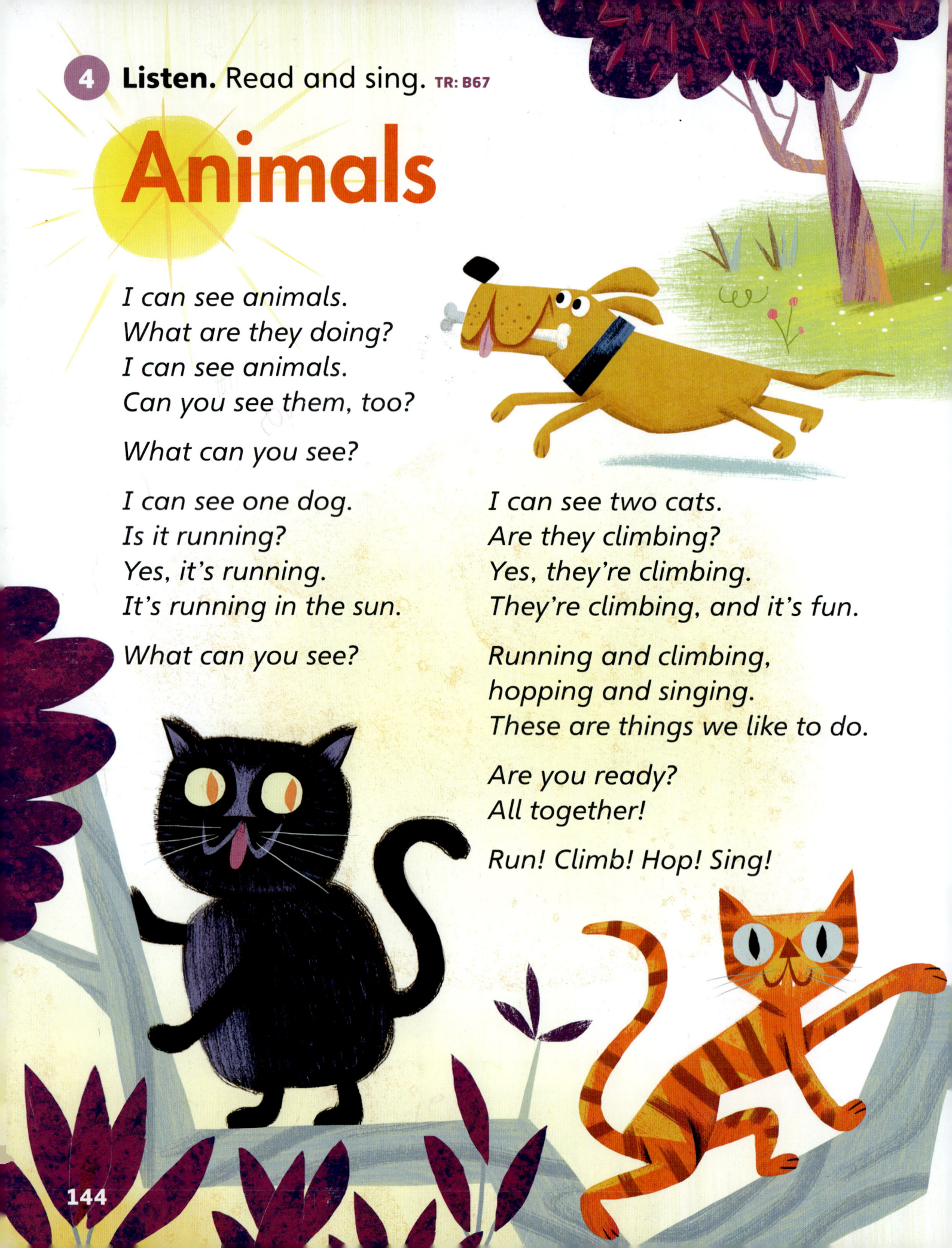

Animals

I can see animals.
What are they doing?
I can see animals.
Can you see them, too?

What can you see?

I can see one dog.
Is it running?
Yes, it's running.
It's running in the sun.

What can you see?

I can see two cats.
Are they climbing?
Yes, they're climbing.
They're climbing, and it's fun.

Running and climbing,
hopping and singing.
These are things we like to do.

Are you ready?
All together!

Run! Climb! Hop! Sing!

What can you see?

I can see three frogs.
Are they hopping?
Yes, they're hopping.
They're hopping on a stone.

What can you see?

I can see four birds.
Are they singing?
Yes, they're singing.
They're singing la, la, la!

La, la, la, la!
La, la, la!

Running and climbing,
hopping and singing.
These are things we like to do.

Are you ready?
All together!
Run! Climb! Hop! Sing!

5 **Sing again.** Hold up pictures.

GRAMMAR TR: B68

What **are** the horses **doing**? They**'re** running.

6 **Listen and find.** Write. TR: B69

1. They're singing 2. They're walking
3. They're sleeping 4. They're running

GRAMMAR TR: B70

Are they **sleeping**? No, they **aren't**.
Are they **eating**? Yes, they **are**.

7 **Listen and find. Circle.** TR: B71

1. sleeping   walking
2. skipping   eating
3. talking   reading
4. sleeping   jumping

8 Listen and say. TR: B72

climb

fly

see

swim

crawl

9 Work with a friend. Point and say.

10 Look. Listen and read. Circle yes or no. TR: B73

1. The birds are flying. yes no
2. The cat is swimming. yes no
3. The insect is crawling. yes no

11 Work with a friend. Listen. Say and stick. TR: B74

Number 1. The dogs are sleeping.

OK. Number 2.

GRAMMAR TR: B75

Do you **want to ride** the donkey?
What **do** you **want to do**?
What **does** Anna **want to do**?

No, I don't.
I **want to ride** the horse.
She **wants to see** the ducks.

12 **Look.** Listen and read. Write. TR: B76

1. Maria ___wants to ride___ the sheep.
2. Carlos ___wants to see___ the frog.

13 **Play a game.** Cut out the cards on page 175. Ask and answer. Play with a friend. TR: B77

Do you want to see the goats?

No, I don't. I want to see the cows.

14 Listen and read. TR: B78

Animal Babies

Who loves babies? Everyone! Let's learn about some animals and their babies. Some animals have big families. Cats have lots of baby cats, called kittens. Baby rabbits are called kittens, too. Baby dogs are called puppies. Baby chickens are called chicks. Some animals, like sheep and elephants, have small families. Baby sheep are called lambs. A baby elephant is called a calf. Everyone loves animal babies!

Baby Asian elephant

15 Listen and read. Look. Circle *yes* or *no*. TR: B79

1. A baby rabbit is called a kitten. yes no
2. A baby sheep is called a chick. yes no
3. A baby elephant is called a calf. yes no

16 Read and write.

Animal Families

cat	dog	chicken	rabbit	sheep	elephant
↓	↓	↓	↓	↓	↓
kitten	Puppies	chick	~~kitten~~	lamb	calf

17 Look and write.

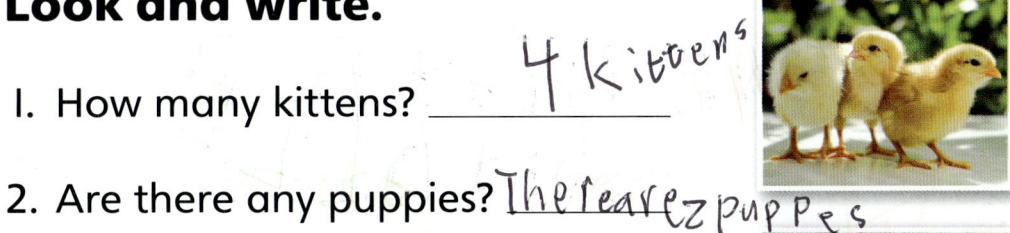

1. How many kittens? 4 kittens
2. Are there any puppies? There are 2 puppies
3. How many lambs? There is 1 lamb
4. Are there any chicks? There are 2 chicks

18 Work with a friend. Ask and answer.
What are your favourite animals? TR: B80

What are your favourite animals?

I like dogs and turtles.

My favourite animal is my cat. Her name is Missy. She is white, brown and grey. Missy has got two kittens. They are so lovely! Boots is black with two white feet. Snowy is all white. I love them all.

19 **Draw and write about your favourite animal.**

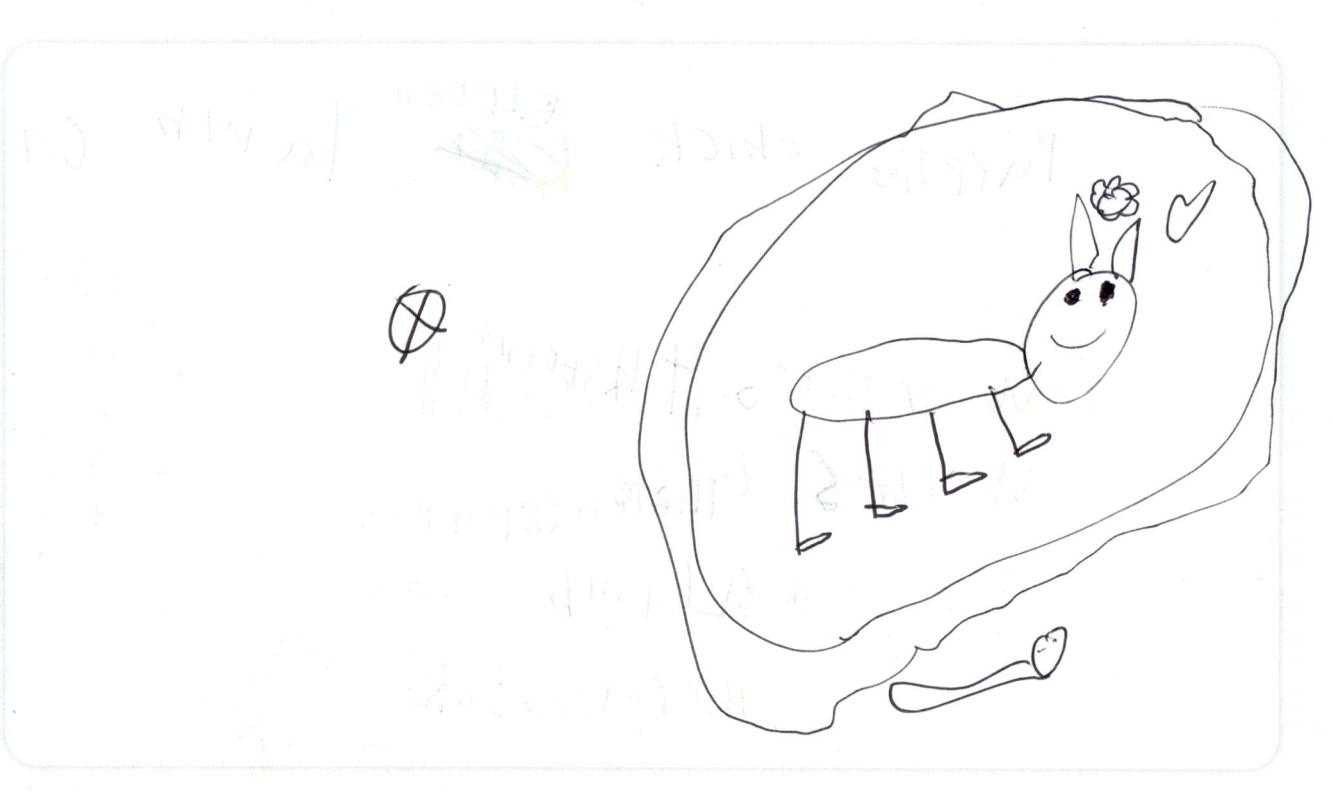

My favourite animal is _Happy_
she likes to hue treats she plays with her ball she sometimees. funny dreams and when she wakes up she barks.

20 **Work in a small group.** Talk about your picture.

NATIONAL GEOGRAPHIC

Our World

Be kind to animals.

21 **Look and read.**

Give your pet food and water.

A hiker and her dog, the Himalayas

22 **Read and copy.**

I am kind to animals.

23 Make a class book about animals.

1. Choose an animal.

2. Glue your picture.

3. Write about your animal.

4. Write your name.

Now I can …

◯ name animals.

◯ talk about what animals can do.

◯ describe my favourite animal.

This is my page. This is a picture of a horse. I love horses.

My favourite animal is a horse. Horses are big and strong. They can run fast.

Anna

Review

Start

Heads = 1 space   Tails = 2 spaces

Work with a friend.
Look. Ask and answer.

Ask a question!

What colour are your eyes?

Finish

157

NATIONAL GEOGRAPHIC OUR WORLD

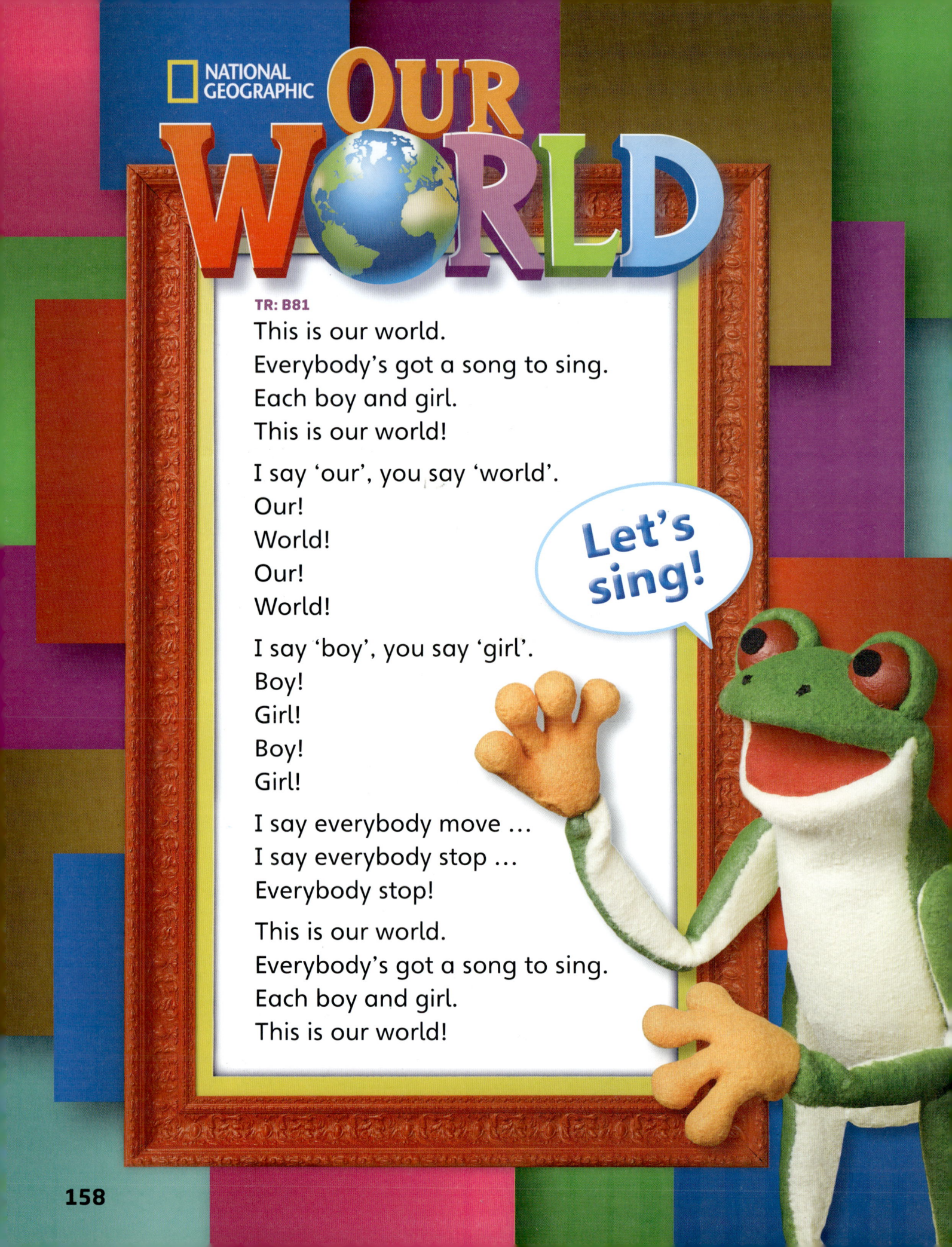

TR: B81

This is our world.
Everybody's got a song to sing.
Each boy and girl.
This is our world!

I say 'our', you say 'world'.
Our!
World!
Our!
World!

I say 'boy', you say 'girl'.
Boy!
Girl!
Boy!
Girl!

I say everybody move …
I say everybody stop …
Everybody stop!

This is our world.
Everybody's got a song to sing.
Each boy and girl.
This is our world!

Let's sing!

Unit 6 Cutouts Use with activity 13 on page 99.

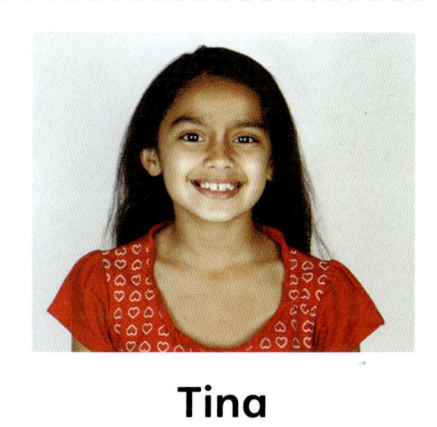

Tina

Tony

Ellen

Ben

169

Unit 7 Cutouts Use with activity 11 on page 117.

171

Unit 8 Cutouts Use with project on page 138.

173

Unit 5
stickers

Unit 6
stickers

Unit 7
stickers

Unit 8
stickers